Polish Joke
and
Other Plays

Other works by David Ives

All in the Timing

Time Flies and Other Short Plays

Monsieur Eek

DAVID IVES

Polish Joke
and
Other Plays

Grove Press
New York

Published simultaneously in Canada
Printed in the United States of America

FIRST EDITION

Library of Congress Cataloging-in-Publication Data

Ives, David.
    Polish joke and other plays / David Ives.
        p. cm.
    Contents: Ancient history—Don Juan in Chicago—The red address—Polish joke.
    ISBN 0-8021-4130-7
    I. Title.
PS3559.V435P65 2004
812'.54—dc22   2003067686

Grove Press
841 Broadway
New York, NY 10003

04 05 06 07 08 10 9 8 7 6 5 4 3 2 1

CONTENTS

PREFACE

This collection brings together four full-length plays I've written over the last dozen years or so: two comedies and two not-so-comedies. The long-one-act version of *Ancient History* in this edition replaces a baggier, two-act version of the play. Casey Childs graciously produced both versions at Primary Stages within the span of just a few years. This new, two-act *Don Juan in Chicago* replaces a baggier three-act version which Casey also produced. *The Red Address,* in the favored tautology of literary managers everywhere these days, "is what it is."

David Ives
August 2003

POLISH JOKE

This play is for Martha, of course

Polish Joke was first presented, at the Ojai Playwrights Conference (Christopher Fields, artistic director) in Ojai, California, in July 2000. The director was Jason McConnell Buzas. The cast was:

JASIU	Kevin Conway
ROMAN, PRIEST	Vic Polizos
WOJTEK, LADISLAW, LEON, MR. O'FLANAGAN, DOCTOR	Victor Raider-Wexler
MAGDA, ZOSIA, ENID, MRS. O'FLANAGAN, NURSE	Nealla Gordon
HELEN, PORTIA, RACHEL, MISS MACFLANAGAN, STEWARDESS	Nancy Bell

Polish Joke was produced at A Contemporary Theatre (Gordon Edelstein, artistic director) in Seattle in July 2001. The director was Jason McConnell Buzas; the scenic designer, Loy Arcenas; the costume designer, Rose Pederson; and the lighting designer, M. L. Geiger.

JASIU	Ted deChatelet
ROMAN, LADISLAW, SANITATION WORKER, KOSCIUSZKO, DOCTOR	Richard Ziman
WOJTEK, PRIEST, POLICEMAN, LEON, MR. O'FLANAGAN	John Aylward
MAGDA, ZOSIA, FLORIST, ENID, MRS. FLANAGAN, NURSE, OLGA	Leslie Law
HELEN, PORTIA, RACHEL, MISS MACFLANAGAN, STEWARDESS	Nancy Bell

5

Polish Joke

Polish Joke was produced in New York at the Manhattan Theatre Club (Lynne Meadow, artistic director) in March 2003. The director was John Rando; the scenic designer, Loy Arcenas; the costume designer, David C. Woolard; the lighting designer, Donald Holder; and the production stage manager, Heather Cousens. The cast was:

JASIU	Malcolm Gets
ROMAN, LADISLAW, SANITATION WORKER, KOSCIUSZKO	Richard Ziman
WOJTEK, PRIEST, POLICEMAN, LEON, MR. O'FLANAGAN, DOCTOR	Walter Bobbie
MAGDA, ZOSIA, FLORIST, ENID, MRS. FLANAGAN, NURSE, OLGA	Nancy Opel
HELEN, PORTIA, RACHEL, MISS MACFLANAGAN, STEWARDESS	Nancy Bell

I would like to thank Jason McConnell Buzas, whose incomparable directorial insights contributed immensely to the creation of this play.

Note: For ease of reading, I have transliterated certain Polish names and words. Except where noted, the name *Sadlowski* is pronounced "Sadlovski." This with apologies to all Poles and Polish speakers.

6

ACT I

A driveway. ROMAN SADLOWSKI *is sitting in a lawn chair with a large, decorated, ceramic beer stein in his hand.* WOJTEK (*pronounced "VOY-tek"*) SADLOWSKI *is deeply asleep in a matching lawn chair.* JASIU (*pronounced "YAH-shoo"*) *is sitting on the ground reading a large black book on whose cover we can read the words "BEING AND NOTHINGNESS." Jasiu is played by an adult actor, but at this point in the play he is nine years old.*

ROMAN *Yah*shoo, today is the feast of Saint Olga. And you are now nine years old.

JASIU I been nine years old for a long time, Uncle Roman.

ROMAN You know what you're gonna be after you're nine, Jasiu?

JASIU I'm gonna be ten.

ROMAN You're gonna be ten. (*Addressing the heavens, lifting the beer stein*) *Now let the great ceremony begin!*

JASIU Uncle Roman, how come you always crack an egg in your beer?

ROMAN I crack a fresh egg in my beer because I'm Polish, Jasiu.

JASIU Is that why you put salt in your beer?

ROMAN Yes, the salt is also Polish. You go all up and down these driveways, you know what the men in those lawn chairs are drinking?

JASIU Beer with eggs and salt?

ROMAN Beer with eggs and salt.

7

JASIU Does beer taste better with eggs and salt?

ROMAN Not really. Eggs and salt is just a part of the Polish heritage. Prob'ly the only Polish discovery besides radium and the sleeveless undershirt.

JASIU Is beer healthier with eggs and salt?

ROMAN There's no rhyme nor reason to this, Jasiu. The tradition is just passed on, like a family curse. Which brings me to a question, now that you are all of nine years old. (*A pause*) Jasiu, do you ever feel like life is totally meaningless?

JASIU I do sometimes, Uncle Roman.

ROMAN Are you sometimes overwhelmed by a tragic feeling of hopelessness and despair?

JASIU I am sometimes.

ROMAN Some days do you get this profound feeling of utter, total futility?

JASIU How did you know that, Uncle Roman?

ROMAN Well, Jasiu, it's complicated.

JASIU Wow . . . !

ROMAN So, off-tentimes I gather you feel defeated and discouraged, disappointed for no good reason?

JASIU Yeah! Lotsa days!

ROMAN Maybe you're doing something personal in the bathroom and a thick black cloud of gloom overwhelms you?

JASIU That happened last Saturday night!

ROMAN And I bet, times like that it's like the universe is empty of purpose. You know that it don't matter what you try, nothin' is ever gonna work out. You know that you're inept. You're a goof, you're a clown, a patsy, a shmo. You know you're gonna die and the great mystery of life will still be unsolved. You'll be on your deathbed gasping out your last, you'll still be looking through the glass darkly.

JASIU I sometimes feel just like that!

ROMAN And this happens maybe two, three times a week?

JASIU Why does that happen to me, Uncle Roman?

ROMAN It's because you're Polish.

JASIU Because I'm Polish?

ROMAN Yes.

JASIU Because I'm *Polish*?

ROMAN Yes. This feeling of meaninglessness and futility? We call this condition the *Polish Gong*.

JASIU The Polish Gong . . . (*We hear a deep gong.*)

ROMAN I take it you have heard the Gong?

JASIU I have heard the Gong! (*We hear the gong again.*) But I'm not just Polish. I'm an American, too.

ROMAN No. Basically, you're Polish. You're just, so to speak, in exile.

JASIU In exile. You mean like Thaddeus Kosciuszko?

ROMAN Like the great Tadeusz Kosciuszko. (*Pronounced "Tah-DAY-oosh Kawsh-CHOOSH-kaw"*) Who came over here and saved America in the Revolution, then went back to save Poland.

JASIU Did he save Poland?

ROMAN   No. Nothing could save Poland.

WOJTEK   (*Waking up groggily in his chair*)   *Okholera* . . . !
(*Pronounced "Aw-khaw-LAY-RA," with a rolled* r; *means, more
or less, "Goddamn it . . ."*)   What time is it?

ROMAN   It don't matter! It's 1365 A.D.! Sleep, Wojtek! Sleep!

WOJTEK   *Okholera* . . . !

Wojtek falls deeply asleep.

ROMAN   Where were we?

JASIU   I'm Polish.

ROMAN   Jasiu, do you know what people call this
neighborhood?

JASIU   The Bush.

ROMAN   The Bush. Here in the Bush we take pigs' guts and
garlic and raw pork and we grind our own sausages.
Springtime, we hang these kielbasas in our living rooms to
dry. We feast on pickled pigs' feet, and tripe, and tongue,
and calf's brains.

JASIU   Well, sure.

ROMAN   Special occasions, we kill a duck and make duck
blood soup with raisins and dumplings.

JASIU   Sure we do.

ROMAN   You're aware, not everybody in America eats these
things. Especially the duck blood soup.

JASIU   I kinda wondered.

ROMAN   Not even the cannibals in *Borneo* eat duck blood
soup. And I bet you heard some Polack jokes in your day.

JASIU   You tell Polack jokes all the time.

ROMAN   You know the word *Polack* is a terrible insult. It's a slap in the Polish face.

JASIU   Dad says I'm not supposed to say "Polack."

ROMAN   Never, ever say "Polack."

JASIU   I won't.

ROMAN   So how many Polacks does it take to screw in a lightbulb?

JASIU   What's a lightbulb.

ROMAN   Correct. Didja hear about the Polack who locked his keys in the car?

JASIU   No.

ROMAN   Took him an hour to get his family out.

HELEN (*O.S.*)   Roman!

ROMAN   Yes, Helen!

HELEN (*O.S.*)   Are you telling Polack jokes?

ROMAN   My godson and me are philosophizing! How's the kielbasa?

HELEN (*O.S.*)   The kielbasa's cooking! Shut up!

ROMAN   Hey, Helen, c'mon out here, give your *swatkeh* a big kiss.

HELEN (*O.S.*)   Stop talking dirty!

WOJTEK (*Waking up groggily as before*)   Okholera . . . !

ROMAN And Jasiu, never say *"okholera."* You know what *okholera* means? It means cholera. It's what your ancestors used to say in the fourteenth century to curse somebody.

JASIU It's bad to say "cholera"?

ROMAN No, it's bad to talk like the fourteenth century when you're living in this one.

WOJTEK *Okholera.* What time is it?

ROMAN It don't matter. Nothing's changed. Sleep, Wojtek! *Spotch! Spotch!* (*Wojtek falls back asleep.*) Where were we?

JASIU Polish jokes.

ROMAN *Polish jokes.* Jasiu, do you know who's the idiot in Shakespeare's *Hamlet?*

JASIU What's *Hamlet?*

ROMAN Polonius is the idiot. In ancient Latin, *Polonius* is Polish for "idiot." Shakespeare, the world's greatest genius, stoops to a Polish joke.

JASIU Why?

ROMAN Well, do you know where the word *Slav* comes from?

JASIU From *Slavic?*

ROMAN No. It comes from *slave.* Because the Slavs were always the slaves.

JASIU Of who?

ROMAN Of whoever was collecting the taxes and kicking our doopa that week. The Russians, the Prussians, the Chinese . . .

JASIU The Chinese?!

ROMAN The *Iroquois* prob'ly kicked our *doopa* for a time. Poland over the ages got sliced and diced so bad, in 1795 Poland disappeared.

JASIU Poland *disappeared*?

ROMAN It vanished for over a hundred years. Like Brigadoon, but without the music. What is this cycle, Jasiu? Why are Polacks the punchline of Western Civilization?

MAGDA *enters. She is wearing a bright red-and-white dress, white shoes, bright red tights, and a rhinestone tiara. Her name is pronounced "MAHG-da," and she too is played by an adult actor.*

MAGDA (*Pronounced "jin DAWB-rih"; means "good morning"*) *Dzień dobry,* Jasiu!

JASIU Hi, Magda.

MAGDA Hiya, Mr. Sadlowski. (*Pronounced "YOK-sha MAHSH"; means "how are you?"*) *Jak się masz?*

ROMAN How are you, Magda.

MAGDA I'm *bardzo dobrze,* thank you. (*Pronounced "BARD-zoe DAWB-zheh"; means "very well"*) You see what I'm dressed like today, Jasiu?

JASIU A Polish flag.

MAGDA A Polish flag. So you wanna play Polish army hospital?

ROMAN Magda, me and Jasiu are having a very important talk right now.

MAGDA On Sundays, Jasiu and me play Polish army hospital.

ROMAN That's wonderful.

MAGDA In the garage.

ROMAN That's wonderf—Wait a minute. *Polish army hospital?*

JASIU Yeah. Magda sorta breaks her footbone.

MAGDA Jasiu sorta fixes it. You see . . .

ROMAN This is wonderful, Magda, but me and Jasiu are talking right now.

MAGDA You know who I'm playing in the Saint Casimir Easter pageant, Mr. Sadlowski?

ROMAN A Polish flag?

MAGDA No, I'm playing the Virgin Mary the mother of God because I got straight A's in conduct. This is the genuine rhinestone tiara I'm gonna wear.

ROMAN Isn't that beauty-ful.

MAGDA You know who Jasiu's playing in the Saint Casimir Easter pageant?

ROMAN The Polish flag?

MAGDA No, he's playing Saint Mary Magdalene.

ROMAN Hold it, hold it. Ain't Saint Mary Magdalene a girl's part?

JASIU I was the only one who fit the wig.

MAGDA Jasiu dresses like a prostitute and dances the "Beer Barrel Polka," then he goes to the Crucifixion and weeps.

ROMAN Magda. Magda. Listen Magda, I'm giving Jasiu some important advice here about being Polish. Good-bye.

MAGDA Don't forget hospital, Jasiu. I think I broke my footbone, doctor. (*Pronouced: "DAW-veed ZEN-ya"; means "see you later"*) *Do widzenia!*

Magda exits.

ROMAN Where the hell was I?

JASIU Polacks are punchlines.

ROMAN *Yes.* Jan Sadlowski, I'm gonna tell you something now that will guide your entire life. Alla the wisdom you ever need to know in just two words.

JASIU Okay.

ROMAN Are you ready?

JASIU I'm ready.

ROMAN All Polish jokes are true.

JASIU Polish jokes are *true?*

ROMAN Yes they are. You know Stanley Bloshchik.

JASIU Sure.

ROMAN You remember how Stasiu—(*Pronounced "STAH-shoo"*)—tried to build his own garage?

JASIU Sure.

ROMAN What happened to Stasiu's garage?

JASIU It fell down.

ROMAN It fell down. What else?

JASIU With Stasiu inside it.

ROMAN With Stasiu inside it. Luckily, Stasiu was building it so bad it didn't kill him when it fell. This is what they call the luck of the Polish. Which means, if the stupid bastard had built his garage right, he'd be dead today. Do you remember Florian Kozwoofski?

JASIU   Sure.

ROMAN   You remember how Florian died?

JASIU   He got hit by a bus.

ROMAN   No. Florian didn't just get hit by a bus. Florian got hit by the bus he was running to *catch*.

JASIU   Was that the luck of the Polish?

ROMAN   Oh, yes. World War Two, the Polish army fought the German tanks on horseback.

JASIU   Was that the luck of the Polish?

ROMAN   It was certainly *testing* the luck of the Polish. You remember Stepan Veetkovski? Hanged himself in his basement and left a suicide note to explain why—and *nobody could read it?*

JASIU   Yeah, well, everything gets spoiled. That's what Mom always says when something happens. Everything gets spoiled.

ROMAN   You know what's the name of the Polish national airline?

JASIU   Is this a Polish joke?

ROMAN   No, I'm asking.

JASIU   I don't know.

ROMAN   You're Polish, you don't know the name of the Polish airline?

JASIU I'm only nine years old.

ROMAN Well the name is *Lot*. What is a "lot"?

JASIU It means "many."

ROMAN No, that's "a lot." I'm talking about your lot in life, your destiny, your fate. Do you think *Lot* is a smart name, do you think people wanna fly on an airplane called *fate*?

JASIU No.

ROMAN Now do you see my point?

JASIU No.

ROMAN Okay. Who lives in alla these houses up and down the block?

JASIU Well, that's Chester and Rita Shishlayvitch, that's Leonard and Yodviga Pshibillchik . . .

ROMAN Do you notice anything about these names?

JASIU They're Polish?

ROMAN No. They're *unpronounceable*. Jasiu, how is a person ever gonna understand life, when are you gonna think when you gotta spend twenty minutes a day spelling your goddamn name for people?

JASIU Sadlowski ain't so bad.

ROMAN You apply for a job with the name Pshibillchik, the boss is gonna panic, he sends you home, he hires Flanagan. Flanagan prospers.

JASIU But our name is Sadlowski.

ROMAN You know Polish is the only world language in which *k* is a vowel? Is there a *k* in Flanagan?

JASIU   I don't think so.

ROMAN   And what do all these unpronounceable guys do for a living?

JASIU   They work in the steel mill.

ROMAN   I work in the mill, your father works *split shift* in the mill—that's why he's in a coma here. What do you want to do when you grow up?

JASIU   I thought I'd work in the mill.

ROMAN   No.

JASIU   Be a janitor?

ROMAN   No.

JASIU   Assistant janitor?

ROMAN   No. No. No.

JASIU   So what *should* I be?

ROMAN   The question is, Jasiu: do you want to be Polish all your life?

JASIU   Well, don't I *have* to be Polish? Since I'm Polish already?

ROMAN   Maybe being Polish is a choice. Or a habit. Or a style. Do I *have* to drink beer with an egg and salt? Am I helpless in the face of my ancestry, just because my parents came from Woodge?

WOJTEK   (*Mumbling in his sleep*)   Woodge . . . ! Woodge. . . !

JASIU   From what?

ROMAN   From Woodge. That's where the family's from. From the city of *Woodge*.

JASIU Woodge . . .

ROMAN *Woodge*—which is spelled *L-O-D-Z.*

JASIU That don't make no sense.

ROMAN So you see my point.

JASIU No.

ROMAN Jasiu, you're gonna find that various nationalities got different traits. Lithuanians, for example, are a loud people, maybe because their country is so small, while Latvians tend to be effeminate—except for the women. Like WASPs.

JASIU "WASPs"?

ROMAN "WASPs" is short for Episcopalians with money. WASPs are not brighter than Polacks, but they got connections. Polacks got no connections, so when we fuck up, we're on our own. The Jews, on the other hand, they got big noses and flat feet but it don't matter, because the Jews are the master race.

JASIU The Jews?

ROMAN Yes. How do I know? Because all women, no matter what their nationality—they get older, they look Jewish.

JASIU Even Aunt Helen?

ROMAN Helen looks more Jewish every day. While men as they get older tend to look more Japanese. Polish people, meanwhile, got a reputation for being backward, stupid, inept, and gloomy.

JASIU So what can I do about being Polish, Uncle Roman?

ROMAN You got to impersonate somebody who is not Polish.

JASIU   How would I do that?

ROMAN   A), you stop talking like a Polack. You get outa this neighborhood and go to a good school and you get some culture. Like Shakespeare and Beathoven.

JASIU   Is that how you pronounce that?

ROMAN   Beathoven. B), you give up the accordion.

JASIU   Give up the *accordion*?

ROMAN   Unless you wanna play Beathoven on it, which is a Polack thing to do. D), stop humming the "Beer Barrel Polka," which is a dead giveaway. E), you change your name to something people can spell, which means G), you pick yourself a good nationality.

JASIU   What nationality should I be?

ROMAN   I dunno, Irish is always good.

JASIU   Why Irish?

ROMAN   The reputation. Everybody loves the Irish. And most important—you can spell their names.

JASIU   Are the Irish smart?

ROMAN   No. But they're crafty. For smart, you gotta go to the Jews. If Einstein had been Polish, he woulda been a janitor all his life. But Einstein was smart enough to be born Jewish.

JASIU   So shouldn't I be Jewish?

ROMAN   That may take powers beyond your control.

JASIU   It's hard to be Jewish?

ROMAN   To be Jewish is an art. To be Irish is a social skill. But to be Polish, Jasiu—that is a *destiny*. And can you escape this destiny? Can you accomplish anything or become somebody in spite of being a Polack? Or will you just get hit by the bus you're running to catch?

JASIU   You mean, maybe there is no escape?

ROMAN   Maybe being Polish is like the human condition itself. And if you're human—how do you escape the human condition?

JASIU   How, Uncle Roman? Tell me.

ROMAN   This will be your investigation. But always, Jasiu, whatever you do—always serve God.

JASIU   I will.

ROMAN   I'm acting as your godfather now. Three days after you were born, I held you in my arms at the baptismal font. I abjured Satan on your behalf. The rest is up to you.

HELEN (*O.S.*)   Roman! The sausage is on the table! Get yer fat doopa in here!

ROMAN   When you get married, Jasiu, always be lovable to your wife.

JASIU   I will, Uncle Roman.

ROMAN   As off-ten as you can. Being lovable is the whole secret of marriage.

WOJTEK (*Waking*)   *Okholera* . . . ! Is there sausage yet?

ROMAN   Alley-oop, brother, it's on the table. (*Wojtek exits.*)   So Jasiu, you remember what I told you today on the feast of Saint Olga.

JASIU I will. Thank you, Uncle Roman.

ROMAN *Now let the great ceremony begin!*

Roman exits. Lights change.

SCENE TWO

An office with two chairs. PORTIA enters.

PORTIA (*Reading from a clipboard*) "John Saydler"?

JASIU John Sadler.

PORTIA Excuse me?

JASIU John Sadler. That is I.

PORTIA So it's pronounced "Sadler," not "Saydler."

JASIU Sadler.

PORTIA Let me see. *S-A* . . .

JASIU . . . *D* . . .

PORTIA . . . *D* . . .

JASIU . . . *L-E-R.*

PORTIA . . . *L-E-R.* "Sadler."

JASIU Just think melancholy. Sad, sadler, sadlest.

PORTIA So there should be two *D*s in "Sadler"?

JASIU No, just one. *S-A-D* . . .

PORTIA Do you mind if I just call you John?

JASIU Please.

PORTIA Phew! That was a workout! How do you do. Welcome to The World Corporation. I'm Portia Benjamin Franklin Hamilton Yale.

JASIU Do you mind if I call you Portia?

PORTIA Actually, I prefer "Miss Yale."

JASIU Ms. Yale.

PORTIA *MISS* Yale.

JASIU Sorry.

PORTIA Just a quirk! Sit down. Anyway, I'm head of human relations here at The World.

JASIU And you're looking for a bright young person, which is I, for a spectacular entry-level position.

PORTIA I have to say the job is fairly spectacular. You—or whoever gets the job—would be our liaison with important international figures representing power, politics, money, power, and money. You would be given a six-figure salary, an office sheathed in Carrara marble, a personal assistant of any gender and sexual orientation you choose, eight weeks' vacation, a fabulous pension plan, and a bag of golf clubs.

JASIU Whew. What about free golf balls for life?

PORTIA Sorry. You have to buy those yourself.

JASIU No thanks!

They laugh politely.

PORTIA What's the matter? Not generous enough?

JASIU Oh, all right, I'll take it.

They laugh politely.

PORTIA Your résumé certainly is wildly impressive. A famous and well-chosen school.

JASIU Yale?

PORTIA Yale. A four-point-one grade average. How did you do that? Degree in literature and philosophy, special study in Shakespeare and . . . ? Pronounce that.

JASIU Beethoven.

PORTIA Summa cum laude, Phi Beta Kappa, National Honors Society. *Mensa.*

JASIU Listen, Mensa asked *me.*

PORTIA Wow. You don't need a job, you need a genius grant.

JASIU All in good time.

They laugh politely.

PORTIA So, John.

JASIU What else can I tell you about myself?

PORTIA What is your nationality?

Jasiu has a sudden prolonged coughing fit.

JASIU I'm sorry. Where were we?

PORTIA "Sodler."

JASIU Sadler.

PORTIA Sadler. What is the nationality of that?

JASIU Why? Do I not *look* like a Sadler?

PORTIA Why don't we say ethnicity interests me.

Polish Joke

JASIU Ethnicity *is* the national pastime.

They laugh politely.

PORTIA You're not related to Bob Sadler, down at the Times?

JASIU Bob Sadler, Bob Sadler . . . No, not to my knowledge, anyway.

PORTIA Maybe Bill Sadler, over at the World Bank?

JASIU Bill Sadler. Nnnnnooooo . . .

PORTIA Barry Sadler, in the State Department?

JASIU Barry Sadler . . .

PORTIA Jewish fella? Flat feet, big nose, dark? Is that your end of the clan?

JASIU Doesn't blow any shofars—so far.

He laughs, she doesn't.

PORTIA What kind of name is that, exactly? "Sadler."

JASIU Some people might say Sadler is an Irish name.

PORTIA *Irish*. Really. Why does Irish somehow surprise me . . .

JASIU (*Sings, with a thick brogue*)
"O Danny boy, the pipes, the pipes are calling!"
Et cetera.

PORTIA That's quite good.

JASIU "From glen to glen and down the mountainside."

PORTIA Wonderful.

JASIU "The summer's gone and all the roses dyin'.
'Tis ye, 'tis ye must go, and I must bide."

PORTIA Oh, don't stop now.

JASIU "But come ye back when summer's in the meadow . . ."
(*He's losing steam, but keeps going.*)
    "Or when the valley's hushed and white with snow . . ."
(*He can't stop himself, though he'd love to stop.*)
    "'Tis I'll be here in sunshine or in shadow.
    O Danny boy . . ." (*No steam at all*)
    "O Danny boy, I love ye so."
    Et cetera. So anyway . . .

PORTIA *Are* you Irish?

JASIU Are *you* Irish?

PORTIA *You're* not Irish.

JASIU Who knows what I am!

PORTIA Your parents never discussed their lineage?

JASIU Mater and pater were pretty tight with their data.

PORTIA Cute.

JASIU So about this job . . .

PORTIA You had no cultural customs as a child? Vibrant clothing, national anthems in unpronounceable languages, disgusting foods . . . ?

JASIU Not that I recall.

PORTIA Did you change your name, John?

JASIU Change my name? Sadler is my name.

PORTIA I mean, originally.

JASIU "Originally."

PORTIA   Originally you were probably . . . what . . .
something . . . Slavic . . . Eastern European . . .
Northeastern European . . . East-of-Germany European . . .
West-of-Lithuania European . . . Maybe . . . Polish?

JASIU   *Polish?*

PORTIA   Yes, I'd say originally Polish. *Are* you Polish?

JASIU   Are *you* Polish?

PORTIA   I? Am I Polish? No. (*Laughs*)   "Am I Polish." No. No.

JASIU   Why is that so funny?

PORTIA   (*Laughs*)   I'm sorry. I'm just laughing at the question.
"Am I Polish?" Oh, that's good.

JASIU   Why is that question funny?

PORTIA   (*Her laughter suddenly stops with a vengeance.*)   Oh, yes,
you think you've got me typed now, don't you. "Portia-
Benjamin-Franklin-Hamilton-Yale"! What a Yankee cliché!
Well, as it happens my ancestors actually landed in the
Mayflower's dinghy. *Do you call that a cliché?*

JASIU   Actually, the dinghy floats it above cliché.

PORTIA   Oh, sure. "Portia Yale." What do we make of that?
Sexless, frigid, repressed, unhip, Upper-East-Side private-
school, junior-year-in-Paris. Why, she probably *tats* of an
evening in some sad apartment full of Jane Austen novels.
Well, you ask my fifteen ex-black boyfriends if I'm frigid!
You ask Rio de Janeiro if I'm repressed! (*Suddenly entirely
rational*)   But where do these stereotypes come from?
Polacks, for example. Any thoughts, John?

JASIU   I don't know. Maybe from Polish jokes.

PORTIA   Polish jokes! For example? (*Before he can even speak*) Did you hear about the Polack who locked his keys in the car? Took him an hour to get his family out. (*Laughs. Stops abruptly*)   Why are you ashamed of being Polish, John?

JASIU   Have I admitted I'm Polish?

PORTIA   "*Have I admitted*" seems to admit that you could be somewhat, if not thoroughly, Polish.

JASIU   Why are you obsessed with national origin, Ms. Yale?

PORTIA   *MISS* Yale!

JASIU   Sorry.

PORTIA   Just a quirk. I see you studied to be a priest in high school. Saint Paul's Seminary. And you're not vaguely Polish? I might have a job for someone vaguely, thoroughly Polish.

JASIU   All right! All right! Yes! Yes! I am.

PORTIA   You are . . . ?

JASIU   I am . . .

He does a little "Polish folk dance" with his feet.

PORTIA   Bisexual?

JASIU   No! I am puh-puh-puh . . .

PORTIA   Polish?

JASIU   Polish.

PORTIA   There! That wasn't so hard, was it?

JASIU   No. What's the big deal? I'm Polish!

PORTIA   You're still a "*human being.*"

JASIU   And I would do a bang-up job in this position.

PORTIA   Yes. Let's talk about the position.

JASIU   Excellent.

PORTIA   There is a small optional quiz.

JASIU   A quiz . . . ?

PORTIA   Totally optional. *Do not feel bad* if you decide not to take the optional quiz. Do you want to take the optional quiz?

JASIU   Of course!

PORTIA   Here we go. Who was the first American president?

JASIU   George Washington.

PORTIA   What is the square root of forty-nine?

JASIU   Seven.

PORTIA   What was your name before you changed it? (*Jasiu goes into a fetal curl.*)   Mr. Sadler? Five, four, three, two . . .

JASIU   Jan Sadlowski.

PORTIA   Sad-LOVE-ski?! Oh, I am so moved.

JASIU   So about this job . . .

PORTIA   You know what a Polish bride gets on her wedding night that's long and hard? *A new last name.* (*Laughs*)   You're not originally Jewish, are you?

JASIU   No.

PORTIA   You're not ashamed of being Jewish, are you?

JASIU   *No.*

PORTIA   You're not ashamed of *not* being Jewish, are you?

JASIU *NO!*

PORTIA Did you play the accordion as a child? Did you make your own sausages? Can you hum the "Beer Barrel Polka"?

JASIU HOW DO YOU KNOW ALL THESE THINGS?

PORTIA Oh, I took a few classes.

JASIU What, Polack recognition classes?

PORTIA For Christ's sake, your name *is* "Sadlowski."

JASIU It's just a name! It's a sound! It's a meaningless squawk produced by air squeezed through vocal cords! That noise has nothing to do with me, or what I am!

PORTIA Of course not. (*Into intercom*) Shonda, would you bring an accordion, please?

JASIU No! No! I will not play the accordion!

PORTIA (*Into intercom*) Shonda, scratch the accordion.

JASIU Can we talk about the job, please?

PORTIA I guess what we're asking is, are there naturally strong and important tribes, like the Romans, and naturally weak and irrelevant tribes, like the Etruscans? Naturally, one can't *say* that.

JASIU Hitler did.

PORTIA One wants to be a Roman and rule, rather than an Estruscan and be eradicated. But if you're born an Etruscan, what the hell do you do about it?

JASIU You tell the Romans to go fuck themselves, that's what you do. Look, I've got nothing to apologize for. I'm not responsible for where my grandparents were born. *I wasn't here!* And I will not be limited by my ethnic background. I will not be told what I am, or what I can be, or what I'm going to be. So why don't you take your entry-level job and enter it up your pedigreed Mayflower dinghy, *MISS YALE!*

PORTIA I like you, Yon. May I call you Yon? Unfortunately, you are up against a fellow named . . . (*Checks a paper*) Flanagan.

We hear the Polish Gong.

JASIU Oh, God . . . Oh, God . . .

PORTIA Irish fella, coincidentally.

JASIU Of course.

PORTIA But, listen, I've had a wonderful time learning about you and your heritage. You know how you sink a Polish battleship?

JASIU Put it in the water.

PORTIA Good-bye, John. And hey—good luck!

Portia exits.

Scene Three

A piece of the floor erupts and LADISLAW appears. He's soiled like a coal miner, in a hard hat and a sleeveless undershirt, and wears a toilet plunger on his belt.

LADISLAW *Okholera* . . . !

JASIU What the . . . !?

LADISLAW (*Sees Jasiu*) *Dzień dobry!*

JASIU *Dzień dobry* . . .

LADISLAW *Jak się masz?*

JASIU *Dobrze, dobrze. . .*

LADISLAW *Dobrze?* You say *dobrze?* I am come from Poland. I am looking for America! You know which way is America?

JASIU This is it.

LADISLAW This is America?

JASIU You're there.

LADISLAW I am here? I am in America? *Oh, Boże, Boże!* (*Pronounced "BAW-zheh"; means "God"*) Thank you! (*He calls down into the hole.*) Zawsha? Zawsha, we are here! We are in America!

ZOSIA'S VOICE (*From inside the hole*) Oh, Boże, Boże, thank you!

LADISLAW Children! Children, we are in America!

CHILDREN'S VOICES (*From inside the hole*) Oh, Boże, Boże, thank you, thank you!

LADISLAW (*Calls into hole*) And all the people here speak Polish!

ZOSIA & CHILDREN'S VOICES (*From inside the hole*) Oh, Boże, Boże, thank you! Thank you!

LADISLAW American mister, your American rock is very hard. Look what it do to good Polish steel. (*He shows a bent pick.*) And Atlantic Ocean? Deeper than I tink.

JASIU You mean you tunneled all the way from Poland?

LADISLAW I tunnel all the way from *Woodge.*

JASIU Woodge?

LADISLAW You know the great city of *Woodge?* Also I bring car, so I can drive in America. This take more time. (*Calls* *into hole)* Zawsha! Honk the horn! (*We hear a car horn.*) You know I lock my keys in car down there, it take me *one hour* to get my family out? *Okholera!* Zawsha, I need beer!

ZOSIA'S VOICE *Proszę!* (*Pronounced "Praw-sheh"; means "coming up!"*)

LADISLAW Children! Put in egg and salt!

CHILDREN'S VOICES *Proszę!*

LADISLAW How are you doing? My name is Ladislaw Sadlowski.

JASIU Did you say . . . ?

LADISLAW Sadlowski. You know some Sadlowskis?

JASIU No. Doesn't ring a gong . . .

LADISLAW You need assistant janitor? I feex your toilet.

JASIU If you'll excuse me . . .

ZOSIA *looks out of the hole.*

ZOSIA So this is America . . . ?

LADISLAW This is America.

ZOSIA (*Crawling out of the hole*) Oh, America is so beautiful!

LADISLAW & ZOSIA (*Sing, to the tune of the "Star-Spangled Banner"*) "Ohh see can yow sigh, by down's eerily liggit . . ."

ZOSIA (*Correcting him*) Lie-git.

LADISLAW Liggit.

ZOSIA Lie-git.

LADISLAW Eugh! American words.

ZOSIA Unpronounceable!

JASIU Excuse me, but why didn't you and your family just fly here?

LADISLAW & ZOSIA *Fly?*

ZOSIA One cannot *fly.*

LADISLAW The bastard Communists! (*He and Zosia spit in disgust.*) Iron Curtain! Berlin Wall! You leave, they kill you!

JASIU Not anymore. The Berlin Wall fell.

LADISLAW *What? It fell?*

ZOSIA The Wall *fell?*

JASIU It fell quite a while ago.

ZOSIA This killed many people? Berlin was very big wall!

JASIU The Communists tore the Wall down.

LADISLAW No! The bastards tore it down?

ZOSIA Children! The bastard Communists tore the Wall down!

CHILDREN'S VOICES *Oh, Boże, Boże,* thank you, thank you!

LADISLAW But what about Poland? What happens to Poland?

JASIU Poland is free.

ZOSIA Free . . . ?! Free . . . ?!

LADISLAW Poland is free?

ZOSIA *O my Poland, you are free!*

JASIU So you could have flown here.

LADISLAW & ZOSIA *Okholera . . . !*

Polish Joke

ZOSIA Ladislaw, what we do now?

LADISLAW Zawsha, we must go back to Poland and fly here!

ZOSIA *Dobrze.* I go pack the children. *Do widzenia!*

JASIU Not if I can help it.

Zosia exits into hole.

LADISLAW Thank you, American mister. If you see some Sadlowskis, you tell them Ladislaw is coming.

JASIU I'll certainly let them know.

LADISLAW God will bless you.

JASIU God will bless me? Really, what for?

LADISLAW For nothing! Because he is God! Is his whole job! *Do widzenia!*

Ladislaw exits into the hole.

JASIU Yeah. Ciao. *Hasta la vista. Wiedersehen.* (*The hole closes up.*) God will bless me. Right.

SCENE FOUR

A classroom with a student's desk and a teacher's book-covered desk. A PRIEST enters, grading a blue book.

JASIU Excuse me, Father.

PRIEST Johannes! Well met, O beloved disciple.

JASIU Have you got a minute?

PRIEST For John Sadlouski? I've got five. ("*Hello and come in*") *Ave atque ingredere.*

JASIU (*"Thank you, Father"*)   *Gratia tibi, Pater.*

PRIEST   You're saving me from the scribblings of Saint Paul's less literate seminarians. *Apostasy* spelled with a *c,* if you can imagine. And this from one of your fellow seniors. Take a pew.

JASIU   Thanks.

PRIEST   Have I told you you're going to be cardinal someday, John?

JASIU   Thank you, Father.

PRIEST   I see a bright red outfit in your future. Cigarette?

JASIU   No thanks.

PRIEST   I won't tell the boss.

JASIU   No, that's okay.

PRIEST   So what brings you to my humble pulpit?

JASIU   Well actually, I've got, like, something on my mind . . .

PRIEST   More to the point, what are you reading outside of class these days?

JASIU   Well—*Hamlet.* For about the fiftieth time.

PRIEST   He did write a couple of other plays, but stick with the Bard. You won't go wrong. What else?

JASIU   Gerard Manley Hopkins.

PRIEST   "Glory be to God for dappled things!" I love it. And?

JASIU   John Donne.

PRIEST   "Batter my heart . . ." Finish.

JASIU   "Batter my heart, three-personed God, for you as yet but knock, breathe, shine, and seek to mend."

PRIEST   They'll make you pope. What else.

JASIU   Ovid, the *Metamorphoses*.

PRIEST   Heaven itself. Have you reached Book Three?

JASIU   Yeah. The part about the fisherman. Amazing!

PRIEST   *"Pauper et ipse fuit . . ."*

JASIU   *". . . moriensque nihil mihi reliquit praeter aquas."*

PRIEST   "My fisherman father too was poor . . ."

JASIU   ". . . and when he died he left me nothing but waters."
Wow!

PRIEST   I never read those lines but I weep. For what does
any father leave us but the waters of life to fish in? The
pagans knew a thing or two about the world. What else is
on your docket?

JASIU   Stendhal.

PRIEST   *Stendhal?* Who gave you Stendhal?

JASIU   *The Red and the Black.* I took it out of the library.

PRIEST   Well, I suppose one Frog novel can't hurt you . . .

JASIU   And I'm finishing *The Brothers Karamazov.* Third time.

PRIEST   I wish this high school had a hundred of you, John.
The Church is embattled. Politics. Gender issues. Female
deities. As if the deity had genitalia. Good Lord. *Freedom of
thought.* A classmate of yours was in here today, he says to me,
Father, why should I sit in a box and confess my sins to you
when I can do that directly with God. I said to him, my boy,
there is a name for that idea. It's called *Protestantism.*

JASIU   Was it Flanagan?

PRIEST Flanagan will go far, the little shit. Pardon my French. You know, we lost forty-two seminarians last year, John. Another forty from your class won't go up to the major seminary after they graduate. I just caught one of your classmates masturbating on the handball court—and *he's* going to be the one with the vocation. I mention no names, but it was Forpucci.

JASIU Father, do you ever regret becoming a priest?

PRIEST Regret . . . ? Well, there are those Saturday nights when it's just you and the pastor singing *The Mikado* together in the rectory. Times like that you start to wonder.

JASIU The thing is . . .

PRIEST You're sure you don't want a smoke?

JASIU No thanks.

PRIEST All right, spill it, John. Come on. What's on the mind.

JASIU It's, um, girls.

PRIEST Girls! Well, that's nice and human. If you'd said sheep or boys, I'd be worried. *Girls.* Good choice. Traditional.

JASIU But it's not just girls, it's like . . . It's girls in red and white.

PRIEST "Girls in red and white." Now that's what I call specific.

JASIU Girls dressed in red and white really, like, I don't know . . .

PRIEST Distract you.

JASIU Yeah. Distract me. Well, no. They really . . .

PRIEST Obsess you.

JASIU Yeah.

PRIEST Is it red-and-white anything in particular? Cheerleader outfits? Leather pantaloons? Rubber aprons?

JASIU No. Just girls in red-and-white anything.

PRIEST Well, as Saint Matthew said—*To each his own.*

JASIU Every time I see a girl dressed in red and white, it's, like, all over. I start shivering, I start sweating . . .

PRIEST Absolutely normal. We've all shivered and sweated in our time. It's human. The *colors* add a certain . . . *je ne sais quoi.*

JASIU See, there was this girl in my neighborhood named Magda. On Sundays she'd wear this red-and-white thing and we'd play Polish army hospital in the garage.

PRIEST Sounds educational. "Polish army hospital . . ." One longs for details.

JASIU Well . . .

PRIEST No matter. No matter.

JASIU Magda'd break her footbone and I'd sort of . . . fix it.

PRIEST How high up did Magda's footbone go?

JASIU All the way up.

PRIEST Ah-ha. If you don't mind—why "army"?

JASIU Because she'd go "*Bang! Bang! Bang!*" while I examined her.

PRIEST   Mm-hm. Quite a war story.

JASIU   The thing is, Magda played the Virgin in our school's Easter pageant.

PRIEST   Mmm. And who did you play in this spectacle?

JASIU   Saint Mary Magdalene.

PRIEST   Mmmm.

JASIU   Magda played Mary, I played Magdalene.

PRIEST   You're getting me worried.

JASIU   She wore white. I wore red.

PRIEST   Deeper and deeper.

JASIU   Then I danced a polka.

PRIEST   Was it the nuns who put you up to this?

JASIU   Sister Mary Seraphim.

PRIEST   They'll fuck us all, the nuns. Pardon my French.

JASIU   I tell you, what really scares me is . . . red and white are the colors of the Polish flag.

PRIEST   Mmm. Does the Polish flag itself arouse you?

JASIU   I haven't really thought about it . . .

PRIEST   Don't bother. Don't bother. You know, John, sometimes there's nothing you can do but pray.

JASIU   I know it's weird.

PRIEST   No. No. We all have our little crimps.

JASIU   Yeah, but isn't this, like, really stupid? And you don't think this is all . . .

PRIEST What.

JASIU ... *because* I'm Polish?

PRIEST Now where did you get this lunatic idea?

JASIU It's like, did I decide to be a priest just because I'm Polish? I mean, who decided? Am I just on some, like, Polish conveyor belt? Eat kielbasa, play the accordion, and on to the priesthood? Maybe it's just, like, fate. Is this my lot?

PRIEST God did not make you Polish, John. He made you a *man*. A human being, unlimited in all eternity. Do the Gospels say Jesus asked the fishermen if they were Polish before he made them his disciples?

JASIU Maybe the Gospels left that out.

PRIEST I won't hear it. It's unhealthy and agnostic. And I don't want to hear the word *fate*. Or *lot*. You have no *lot*. For God's sake, you've got all the world before you! You've got a good mind. A good heart. A vocation to the priesthood. You just have a curious ... chromatic problem at the moment. There's a purpose to everything in life, and girls in red and white are obviously your test.

JASIU Pretty stupid test.

PRIEST Let's just pray we're all graded on the curve. But amen amen, I say unto you, the girls in red and white too shall pass.

JASIU I don't think so.

PRIEST Just wait till Theology up at the major seminary. *Transsubstantiation*. That'll KO the old red and the white.

JASIU The thing is ...

PRIEST Aquinas will clear your head like horseradish.

JASIU The thing is, Father, I won't be going up to the major seminary. I'm leaving Saint Paul's.

PRIEST No, John.

JASIU Yeah. I'm transferring out tomorrow.

PRIEST No, John.

JASIU Yes, Father.

PRIEST Why? And why so fast? It's not just the girls in red and white, is it?

JASIU No . . .

PRIEST Then why, for God's sake?

JASIU Well. I've lost my vocation.

PRIEST Oh, a temporary lapse, maybe. We all have moments of doubt . . .

JASIU No, it's gone.

PRIEST Not *gone* . . .

JASIU Yes. Yes. My vocation is gone. I know because every day at Mass I'd, like, check for it. Just like you check for your wallet. It was always right here. (*The middle of his chest*) Like this invisible thing I carried around. Right in here. Like this flame. Then one day I was kneeling there in chapel and it was gone. The flame was out. You know how you reach for your wallet and your pocket's empty and you get that panicky feeling, you check all your pockets, but you know your wallet's gone already—? Stolen? My vocation was gone and I was hollow, right here, all the way back. There was just . . .

PRIEST A void.

JASIU A void. It's been like that for weeks and weeks.

PRIEST As I say, John . . .

JASIU I've prayed, Father. I swear. I've prayed every day.

PRIEST I see.

JASIU It's like I had this great ticket in that wallet. I was headed for this wonderful place. I was going to be something so wonderful. But God took the ticket back. Why would God do that?

PRIEST I don't know.

JASIU It's not like I did anything. Did I throw it away somehow? What did I do? How did I lose this?

PRIEST It wasn't *you* . . .

JASIU I love this school, Father. I've never loved anything like this school. I love your class.

PRIEST There's no need for haste, you know. You could wait for the end of the school year . . .

JASIU Oh, *fuck,* Father. Fuck. Shit. Fuck. Fuck.

PRIEST Keep going. Fuck.

JASIU Fuck. Fuck. Fuck.

PRIEST Well, John . . . Fuck. Better you found this out now than after ordination. Though I had hoped we'd be singing *The Mikado* together some night as fellow curates.

JASIU I'm sorry, Father. I'm real sorry.

PRIEST You've got nothing to apologize for, lad.

JASIU I feel so bad. So empty.

PRIEST And that too will pass.

JASIU I don't think so. My mother always says, *"Everything gets spoiled."*

PRIEST Virgil says, *"Forsan et haec olim meminisse iuvabit."* "Someday we will look back on these things—and we will laugh."

JASIU Maybe what he meant was, someday we'll see the joke's on us.

PRIEST Well, that's too atheistical for me.

JASIU Maybe I'm an atheist.

PRIEST I think you'd better stop reading *Hamlet.* It's a great play but a hell of a role model. Well, I'm only saying all this to keep you here a minute longer.

JASIU Good-bye, Father.

PRIEST Good-bye, John. Always remember: knowledge. Inquiry. The life of the mind.

JASIU Yes, Father.

PRIEST Come visit us sometime.

JASIU I will.

PRIEST You write me.

JASIU I will. I will. (*Priest exits. A cell phone rings. Jasiu takes out a cell phone and speaks into it.*) Hello? Rachel—hi! Yeah, I'm on my way . . . Listen, Rachel, I can't talk right now, I'm in a theater. I'll be right there, I just have to pick something up. I love you too. 'Bye!

SCENE FIVE

A florist shop. The tinkle of a bell over a shop door as Jasiu goes into it. A FLORIST enters, carrying a bouquet and humming "Danny Boy."

JASIU   Hi there. Good evening. Are you still open? I'm in kind of a hurry, I'm running late for a party . . . *(Paying Jasiu no attention, the Florist exits, as if she hadn't heard or seen him.)*   Hello? Excuse me? Miss? Hello? I'm on my way to a . . . *(Florist reenters, still not paying Jasiu any attention.)*   Hi there, I'm in kind of a rush. My girlfriend's throwing a party and I need . . . a bouquet of some kind . . . *(Florist exits.)*   I'm actually supposed to be at that party right now . . . Hello? Hello? *(Florist reenters.)*   Hello?

FLORIST   *(Screams, noticing Jasiu)*

JASIU   Sorry.

FLORIST   Jesus, you scared me.

JASIU   Sorry. I'm sorry.

FLORIST   Is there something I can do for you?

JASIU   Yes, my girlfriend's throwing a party and I need a nice bouquet.

FLORIST   Have you ever thought about emigrating?

JASIU   Excuse me?

FLORIST   Emigrating? Leaving America, going someplace where you can actually be somebody?

JASIU   What are you talking about? Emigrating?

FLORIST   Yeah. Leaving America and going someplace where you can—

JASIU I know, I know what emigrating means. I just want some flowers for this party.

FLORIST (*Calling out as if he wasn't there*) Hello? Hello? Sir? Sir—?

JASIU I'm right here!

FLORIST Sorry. I lost sight of you there for a second.

JASIU I've been standing right here for five minutes trying to buy some flowers.

FLORIST So what can I do for you? Passport? Airline ticket?

JASIU *Some flowers.* Maybe something for about fifty dollars?

FLORIST Fifty dollars. You're making things too easy. (*She produces a tiny, pathetic, dry bouquet.*) There you go. We call this arrangement "Ukrainian Spring."

JASIU That's fifty dollars?

FLORIST Plus tax. Say, do I know you from somewhere?

JASIU I don't think so.

FLORIST Yeah, I know you, I know you from somewhere.

JASIU Well, I wrote a highly acclaimed novel, maybe you . . .

FLORIST No, no, no, I don't waste my time with novels.

JASIU I've published some poetry.

FLORIST Does anybody still write poetry?

JASIU I do.

FLORIST Well I know I know you from someplace. *HELLO? HELLO? SIR—?*

JASIU I'm right here.

FLORIST   Give a shout from time to time, let me know you're still there.

JASIU   I'm standing right here.

FLORIST   So what can I do for you?

JASIU   Some *FLOWERS*, please. *Flowers.*

Shop bell tinkles and a SANITATION WORKER enters in filthy overalls, wiping his face with a banana peel.

SANITATION WORKER   Hey there.

FLORIST   Good evening, sir. Welcome!

SANITATION WORKER   Wow. Lotta garbage out there. What a night for refuse.

The Worker walks right at Jasiu as if he's not there.

JASIU (*Stepping aside to let the Sanitation Worker by*)   Sorry.

FLORIST   So can I help you, sir?

JASIU   Yes, I still want that . . .

SANITATION WORKER   Yeah, I'm looking for a bookay for a stag party. I'm running kinda late here, I got my garbage truck parked outside.

JASIU   Excuse me, but I've been standing here . . .

FLORIST (*Speaking to a place where Jasiu is* not *standing*)   Just one moment, please, sir. I'm dealing with this gentleman.

SANITATION WORKER   You got some nice buds for maybe five bucks?

FLORIST   Five dollars? You're making it too easy. (*She produces an enormous, gorgeous bouquet.*)   There you go. We call this "Irish Summer."

SANITATION WORKER Beauty-ful! I'll take it. (*The Worker pays for the flowers with a fish as he and the florist hum "Danny Boy."*) You know, I had a very curious dream last night.

FLORIST You had a curious dream?

SANITATION WORKER A very curious dream. It was all in Gaelic.

FLORIST Do you speak Gaelic?

SANITATION WORKER No!

FLORIST Are you Gaelic yourself?

SANITATION WORKER No! I'm not even half Gaelic!

FLORIST That is very curious.

JASIU Look, this is really impossible—

FLORIST (*Again addressing a spot where Jasiu is not standing*) Yeah, yeah, yeah, your girlfriend's throwing a party. What's her name?

JASIU What?

FLORIST Your girlfriend, what's her name?

JASIU What's the difference what her name is?

FLORIST She doesn't have a name?

JASIU Her name is Rachel.

FLORIST Rachel. And you want to impress *Rachel* with some flowers. Now will you wait your turn, please? (*To Worker*) So you had this curious dream . . .

SANITATION WORKER So in this dream it's nighttime and I'm in a flowershop buying some flowers for a party.

48

FLORIST Weird.

SANITATION WORKER At which point, a bell rings, and a mysterious woman enters the shop.

Shop bell tinkles as a WOMAN *enters, dressed in black from head to foot and wearing a hat with a long black veil. She walks right at Jasiu.*

JASIU (*Stepping aside to let the Woman by*) Sorry.

SANITATION WORKER She's dressed all in black and she has a black veil and she's weeping uncontrollably. (*Woman weeps uncontrollably.*) Piteously. (*Woman weeps piteously.*) In anguish.

FLORIST In Gaelic?

SANITATION WORKER In Gaelic.

WOMAN IN BLACK *Erin go bragh!*

SANITATION WORKER At which point, the mysterious woman buys a bouquet, something called, um . . . what was it . . .

JASIU Irish Summer.

SANITATION WORKER (*Pays no attention*) . . . what was it? . . .

FLORIST Irish Summer?

SANITATION WORKER Irish Summer! (*The Florist produces another gigantic bouquet and hands it to the Woman, who turns to leave and* screams *when she sees Jasiu.*) Then she screamed.

FLORIST In Gaelic?

SANITATION WORKER I think it *was* Gaelic.

JASIU (*Stepping aside for the Woman*) Sorry! (*Mysterious woman exits; shop bell tinkles.*)

FLORIST That is a very curious dream. Was there a clock?

SANITATION WORKER   Yes! I didn't mention the curious clock on the wall, shaped like a sausage and garlic.

A clock shaped like a garlic with phallic sausage hands flies in.

FLORIST   Was the garlic Gaelic?

SANITATION WORKER   It was Gaelic garlic!

FLORIST   You know I had a curious dream myself last night. I was in the Warsaw production of *The Invisible Man*—

JASIU   *I had a dream that I got some service in a goddamn FLOWER SHOP.*

The Florist and Sanitation Worker turn to him.

SANITATION WORKER   Did you say something, buddy?

JASIU   You know, I'm a blue-collar person myself. Originally.

SANITATION WORKER   What are you trying to imply, some kinda kinship here?

FLORIST (*Into telephone*)   Hello? 911? We got a problem here.

JASIU   No, no, it's okay, it's okay.

SANITATION WORKER   Hey, hey, hey, do I know you from somewhere?

FLORIST   Yeah, he wrote some novel.

SANITATION WORKER   I don't waste my time with novels. I read poetry.

JASIU   I've written some poetry.

SANITATION WORKER   That's it! That's how I know you!

JASIU   You know my poetry?

SANITATION WORKER   No, you're the janitor in my building! Are you the assistant janitor in my building!

FLORIST   He's a fucking poet!

SANITATION WORKER   This guy's the assistant janitor in my building!

JASIU   I do manage some real estate for a living but actually I'm a writer . . .

SANITATION WORKER   Hey, fix my toilet when I get a chance, will ya?

JASIU   I don't fix toilets.

SANITATION WORKER   Obviously not, it's been broke for months!

Shop bell tinkles as POLICEMAN *enters.*

POLICEMAN   I'm Officer Gaelic. Is there some kinda problem here?

FLORIST   Yeah, this *poet* is trying to buy some flowers.

POLICEMAN   Did he try to buy the Irish Summer?

SANITATION WORKER   Yeah!

POLICEMAN   Did he offer you fifty dollars?

FLORIST   Yeah!

SANITATION WORKER   And he tried to cut in line!

JASIU   Now wait a minute . . .

POLICEMAN   I'll talk to you in a minute, Shakespeare.

FLORIST   I told him to emigrate. He wouldn't listen.

POLICEMAN   Resisting emigration, eh. Any witnesses?

Woman in black enters.

WOMAN IN BLACK   I'm a witness. I saw the whole thing.

POLICEMAN   Now who're you?

WOMAN IN BLACK   I'm a mysterious woman in black. And that man—(*Pointing at Jasiu*)—is trying to pass.

POLICEMAN   Trying to pass, eh. For what he's not?

SANITATION WORKER   This yahoo can't pass for what he's not.

JASIU   *Jasiu.*

FLORIST   He's a nonentity already!

WOMAN IN BLACK   He's trying to pass for what he *is*.

POLICEMAN   Impersonating himself, is he.

SANITATION WORKER   Deport the son of a bitch!

FLORIST   Send him to the mill!

WOMAN IN BLACK   Send him to Woodge!

WORKER, FLORIST, & WOMAN (*A lynch mob, chanting*)   *Woodge. Woodge. Woodge. Woodge.*

POLICEMAN   All right, all right, HOLD IT! (*They go silent.*)   Okay, bud. Explain yourself.

JASIU   Well, Officer, it's really very simple. (*Polish Gong. The others exit, leaving Jasiu. He speaks to us.*)   *I* once had a curious dream. I dreamt that I was born into a Polish settlement in a large American city, and my dream name was Jan Bogdan Sadlowski. And in my dream I had Polish parents and went to a Polish school where we sang Polish songs. And all these things seemed completely normal to me—maybe because everybody around me was having the same dream I was. Or maybe because my dream was indistinguishable from real life. And at the heart of the heart of my dream there was a terrible hunger and a dissatisfaction, as if I was running from something. And I knew what I was running from but not what I was looking for. And then in my dream I ran into a wonderful girl named Rachel who for some reason loved me . . . I was on my way to see her, but I was in the wrong part of town. I was in a flower shop but I couldn't buy any flowers. And I had a bus to catch, so I ran out into the street, where the lights of my bus were shining in the distance. (*Lights change to a spotlight on Jasiu.*)   I started to chase it. The night was dark all around me but I kept running. And I ran and I ran and I cried out, *Wait! Wait! That's my bus!* And as the headlights of the approaching bus burned into the back of my brain, two things hit me right between the eyes. First, an amazing revelation, the answer to all my problems. Second—the bus.

Blackout.

End of Act I.

ACT II

Scene One

A foyer. Jasiu stands bent, out of breath.

JASIU (*Gasping*)   Oh my God. Oh my God.

RACHEL (*O.S.*)   Jack . . . ? (RACHEL *enters.*)   Jack, where have you been? Everybody's here.

JASIU (*Numbly*)   Hi, Rachel. Hi.

RACHEL   What is it? Jack, what's the matter?

JASIU   Jesus. . . !

RACHEL   What's the matter? What happened?

JASIU   Well, I was coming here . . . I was running late . . .

RACHEL   What happened?

JASIU   I got hit by a bus.

RACHEL   No! Hit by a . . . ?

JASIU   A bus. It bashed me in the shoulder, threw me in the street . . .

RACHEL   Are you all right? Are you hurt?

JASIU   No, I'm fine. But that's not all.

RACHEL   Are you hurt?

JASIU   No, that's not all, Rachel. This bus that hit me? It was the bus I was running to catch.

RACHEL (*A moment; then she finds that funny.*)   Oh, sweetie . . .

JASIU   Rachel—*it was the bus I was running to catch.* Do you see?

54

RACHEL Well, it was the bus you wanted. I'd call that good timing.

JASIU No, I'd call that a Polish epiphany. A streetcar called Getoutatown.

RACHEL Don't even start.

JASIU I was going to bring some flowers but I couldn't *get* any flowers.

RACHEL It's okay, it's okay. All is well. Come on in.

JASIU But *that's* not all, Rachel. That's not the important part.

RACHEL Of course not, how could it be?

LEON *enters.*

LEON Don't tell me. Jack Sadler.

JASIU Yes. Hello . . .

LEON You're the Jack Sadler I've been hearing so much about.

JASIU If I am, half of it's probably true.

LEON I'll take the good half.

RACHEL Jack, this is Leon. Dad—this is Jack.

JASIU How do you do, sir.

LEON Late for your own party? My Rachel was having *shpilkis.*

JASIU Ah-ha. I'm sorry?

LEON Rachel was having *shpilkis.*

JASIU Oh. Were they good?

LEON   *Shpilkis! Shpilkis!*

RACHEL   Nerves.

JASIU   Ah-ha.

LEON   "Were they good." That's good.

JASIU   Well, I had some raspberry *shpilkis* the other day. Very tasty.

LEON (*Laughs*)   So what do you do for a living, Mr. Jack Sadler? My Rachel's been mysterious.

JASIU   I run the World Bank.

LEON   That's a nice job. Can you lend me a little till Tuesday? (*Laughs*)   So what do you really do?

RACHEL   Dad, I told you about Jack's schooling and everything. The wonderful novel he wrote.

LEON   My Rachel's got this *fakockteh* idea she likes you somehow.

JASIU   I had hoped to be a high-level figure in power, politics, and money, but what I really do is—I'm a janitor.

RACHEL   Jack isn't a janitor. He manages some very large buildings.

LEON   Real estate. Very nice.

JASIU   No, I'm a high-level assistant janitor.

RACHEL   He's a writer is what he is.

JASIU   You know—toilets, garbage, are the halls clean.

LEON   Ah-ha.

RACHEL   He's exaggerating, of course.

LEON Well, you've got no place to go but up.

JASIU Yeah. Maybe they'll make me elevator operator. (*Leon laughs.*) It'd give me more time to read Wittgenstein.

LEON Wittgenstein . . .

RACHEL He's even got me reading the stuff. Oh, it's *fun*.

LEON Well, Mr. Jack Sadler, I've got a couple of people here I'd like you to meet . . .

RACHEL Dad—Dad, could I catch up with Jack alone for a second?

LEON Sure, sure. I'll talk to you some more, Mr. Sadler. Welcome.

Leon exits.

RACHEL Jack, was that the best you could do?

JASIU Listen . . .

RACHEL Talk to him! He's a great guy!

JASIU About what? Septic systems maybe?

RACHEL You are not a janitor.

JASIU But that's part of the epiphany! Listen. The bus lights are heading toward me, what do I realize? *I am a janitor.* Think about it. Jan Sadlowski. How do you spell "Yon"? *J-A-N.* What does janitor begin with? *J-A-N.* I say I'm a writer. I even say I manage buildings. But I'm a high-level guy with a toilet plunger. But I'm not going to be one for long. That's part of the revelation too.

RACHEL You know, I like you even though you can be like this.

ENID *enters.*

ENID So this is him? So *this* is *him*? Oh, *yes*! Beautiful! Perfect! Oh, Rachel, congratulations, let me take a picture of you two for posterity.

RACHEL Jack, this is my cousin Enid.

ENID For how many years I said to Rachel, get yourself a nice Jewish guy, and now look what happens!

RACHEL Yeah, look what happens.

JASIU Yeah! Look what happens!—What happened?

ENID She finds him! And so beautiful! Can I say that, Rachel? He is *gorgeous*. *And* Jewish. Can I steal him for a weekend? Please?

JASIU You know, Enid, I think you've been misinformed.

ENID She's crazy for you, you know.

JASIU I know. But I'm not Jewish.

An embarrassed pause.

ENID I'm sorry. I'm so, so sorry.

RACHEL Anyway, what's the difference?

ENID Right! What's the difference?

JASIU You still want that weekend away with me?

ENID I'm so embarrassed.

JASIU Can I offer you some *shpilkis*?

ENID I've got some of my own, thank you. But if you don't mind my asking . . .

JASIU I'm Irish.

RACHEL No, he's not.

Polish Joke

JASIU I'm Irish.

RACHEL He's not Irish.

JASIU A 100 percent, full-blooded, pedigreed lace-curtain Mick.

ENID Somehow I thought you were Polish. You know, Polish-slash-Jewish.

JASIU Not Polish, not Jewish.

RACHEL Not Irish, either.

ENID Maybe I should let you two work this out. Nice meeting you, Jack. And I'm so, so sorry.

JASIU *Shalom!* (*Enid exits. Jasiu calls after her.*) Sorry I'm not Jewish!

RACHEL Listen, Jack . . .

JASIU You didn't tell her I wasn't Jewish?

RACHEL I didn't tell her you *were* Jewish! I didn't tell her anything! She just read into you.

JASIU What am I, a Rorschach blot?

RACHEL According to you, you're Irish.

JASIU Yeah, Irish with the luck of the Polish.

RACHEL Listen. Come in and meet the wonderful guests. Have a drink. I'll stand on a chair and say, ladies and gentlemen, here he is, a non-Jewish janitor but you're gonna love him anyway even though he reads Wittgenstern.

JASIU Wittgenstein.

RACHEL You say Toledo, I say Tolaydo.

JASIU Rachel, I don't belong here. I don't belong in this world. I mean, the *world*, the big world, the modern world, any world.

RACHEL You are in a state, aren't you.

JASIU Yeah. But not the state I belong in. But you know what? I know the answer now.

RACHEL So do I.

JASIU That's what I'm trying to tell you. I know the solution to all my problems. It's wild, it's crazy, it's baroque, but it's the Big-A Answer. Listen to this.

RACHEL Come into the party, Jack. Come out of the foyer and into the frying pan. I promise, I promise, you'll love it.

She kisses him.

JASIU Your father wants you. He's signaling.

RACHEL Please, Jack.

JASIU You go in. I'll be in in a minute.

RACHEL The water's fine, dive right in.

Rachel exits.

JASIU I know the answer.

He puts on a green wool "Irish" cap.

SCENE TWO

A travel agency. Impossibly beautiful travel posters of Ireland appear as MR. O'FLANAGAN enters. In a green jacket and hat, he recalls a leprechaun.

Polish Joke

MR. O'FLANAGAN (*The thickest Irish brogue you ever heard*) Top o' the mornin' to ye, sar!

JASIU Top o' the mornin'.

MR. O'FLANAGAN Top o' the mornin' and what a fine and lovely mornin' it is too, begosh. Why sure the sun is baymin' upon us like the smile of a buxom Irish farm lass tuggin' a Guernsey's udders at daybreak. And what can the Erin Go Bragh Travel Agency be after doin' for ye this fine and lovely mornin', sar?

JASIU I'd like to book a ticket to Ireland, please.

MR. O'FLANAGAN Bookin' a thrip to the ould emerald sod, are we? Sure isn't that a darlin' thing to be doin' on a fine and lovely day like today when the air is as sweet as the milk off the swollen teat of a new mother nursin' her babe on a sunny afternoon in June. Are ye goin' over for a holiday, or do ye have . . . a family connection?

JASIU Well, let me put it this way. I'd like a *one-way* ticket, please.

MR. O'FLANAGAN One way, sar? Now don't be after tellin' me . . . But you couldn't be . . . ?

JASIU Yes. I'm moving to Ireland.

MR. O'FLANAGAN Jaysus be praised! Movin' to Ireland! Why sure just the hearin' o' that makes me heart flop about inside me like a new-caught salmon in a fisherman's basket in Killarney at about 6:35 P.M. on a Tuesday in July. Miss MacFlanagan! Miss MacFlanagan, would ye come in here, please?

MISS MacFLANAGAN *enters, a perfect Irish colleen.*

MISS MACFLANAGAN Are ye after callin' me, Mr. O'Flanagan?

MR. O'FLANAGAN Is that you then, Miss MacFlanagan?

MISS MACFLANAGAN Aye, 'tis I, Mr. O'Flanagan.

MR. O'FLANAGAN Top o' the mornin' to ye, Miss MacFlanagan.

MISS MACFLANAGAN And top o' the mornin' to you, Mr. O'Flanagan.

MR. O'FLANAGAN This here is Miss MacFlanagan, sar.

MISS MACFLANAGAN Top o' the mornin', sar.

JASIU Top o' the mornin'.

MR. O'FLANAGAN And a hearty top o' the mornin' to us all. Why sure it makes me feel so fine and lovely to say it, why don't we all say it again. Top o' the mornin'!

MISS MACFLANAGAN Top o' the mornin'!

JASIU Top o' the mornin'!

MISS MACFLANAGAN And what a fine and lovely and grand mornin' it is too. Why the sky is as blue as the eye of a freckle-faced Irish bishop squeezin' the cheeks of the choir on Pentecost. Wouldn't ye say, sar?

JASIU Yes. Yes. It certainly is. I mean . . . (*Brogue*) Why sure the air is after bein' as fresh and sweet as the dew-suckin' daffodils on the south side of the Hill of Howth in the turd week of May.

MISS MACFLANAGAN And sure don't it make ye want to hoover in the succulent oxygen of the ould country again?

MR. O'FLANAGAN Aye, sure that it does, Miss MacFlanagan.

MISS MACFLANAGAN   Aye, sure.

JASIU   Aye, sure.

MR. O'FLANAGAN   Aye, sure. But look ye, Miss MacFlanagan, here's a darlin' gentleman who's after bookin' a *one-way passage* to the fine and lovely and grand and happy-go-lucky isle of Ireland.

MISS MACFLANAGAN   Sure ye're not after sayin' that, Mr. O'Flanagan?

MR. O'FLANAGAN   After and before, begosh. Why, the darlin' gentleman's after movin' there!

MISS MACFLANAGAN   Jaysus be praised! Then I tink we better be after tellin' Mrs. Flanagan.

MR. O'FLANAGAN   Mrs. Flanagan! Mrs. Flanagan, would ye be after comin' in here, please?

MRS. FLANAGAN *enters.*

MRS. FLANAGAN   Are ye after callin' me then, Mr. O'Flanagan?

MR. O'FLANAGAN   Is that you then, Mrs. Flanagan?

MRS. FLANAGAN   Sure and who the feck else would it be, after answerin' to the name of Flanagan? But a top o' the mornin' to ye!

MR. O'FLANAGAN   Top o' the mornin', Mrs. Flanagan!

MRS. FLANAGAN   And top o' the mornin' to you, Miss MacFlanagan.

MISS MACFLANAGAN   And top o' the mornin' to you, Mrs. Flanagan!

MR. O'FLANAGAN   And here's a darlin' gentleman by the name of . . . ?

Pause.

JASIU (*A decision*) Jack Flanagan.

MR. O'FLANAGAN *Jack Flanagan* is it?

MISS MACFLANAGAN Jaysus be praised!

MRS. FLANAGAN It's a relation!

MR. O'FLANAGAN Mr. Flanagan, this here is Mrs. Flanagan.

JASIU Top o' the mornin', Mrs. Flanagan!

MRS. FLANAGAN Top of the mornin', Mr. Flanagan!

MISS MACFLANAGAN Did I say top o' the mornin'?

MRS. FLANAGAN Top o' the mornin'!

MISS MACFLANAGAN Top o' the mornin'!

MR. O'FLANAGAN Well, I tink that's enough o' "top o' the mornin'" for today.

MRS. FLANAGAN And isn't it a fine and lovely and grand and blessed day too.

MR. O'FLANAGAN Oh, aye.

MISS MACFLANAGAN Aye.

JASIU Aye, aye.

MRS. FLANAGAN Sure isn't the breeze today as fine and lovely and grand and blessed as the first good fart after a plate o' cooked cabbage.

JASIU, MR. O'FLANAGAN, & MISS MACFLANAGAN Aye, aye.

MRS. FLANAGAN And sure don't the golden honeyed light just smarm yer whole bein' like a first-rate fook in the barn on Christmas mornin'?

JASIU, MR. O'FLANAGAN, & MISS MACFLANAGAN Aye, aye, aye . . .

MRS. FLANAGAN And isn't it a feckin' fair and handsome man I'm looking at, too. As stout and hard as the paynis on a champion racehorse at studtime.

JASIU Aye, aye. A stout hard paynis, begosh. Aye, aye, aye, aye . . . (*He realizes the other two aren't joining in.*) Aye.

MR. O'FLANAGAN Well, that's the weather for today. But look ye, Mrs. Flanagan, Mr. Flanagan here is after movin' to—guess where.

MRS. FLANAGAN O Jaysus be praised but he's a looky bastard.

MR. O'FLANAGAN He's a looky bastard indayd.

MRS. FLANAGAN A happy bastard.

MR. O'FLANAGAN A happy bastard.

MRS. FLANAGAN A happy-go-lucky bastard.

MR. O'FLANAGAN A happy-go-lucky bastard.

MISS MACFLANAGAN And a Flanagan.

MR. O'FLANAGAN And a Flanagan.

MISS MACFLANAGAN Why sure I'd marry the darlin' man this moment but that I'm engaged to a fisher lad who's out on the moanin' sea right now. And till a cruel hard storm comes up and Michael MacMcFlanagan's bloated and stinkin' corpse washes up on MacFishbellybelly Strand, sure I'm not free just yet.

MRS. FLANAGAN Well, there's hope for ye, Miss MacFlanagan. For sure a storm is brewin' and soon we'll be happily keenin' together over the putrid remains of Michael MacMcFlanagan on the sands of MacFishbellybelly Strand.

MR. O'FLANAGAN But Mr. Flanagan, before ye take this young widow in holy matrimony, tell me in sooth: Why are ye movin' back to the land of your sainted ancestors? Is it the pot o' gold ye're after seekin'?

JASIU All that I seek is happiness.

MISS MACFLANAGAN Happiness. Aye.

MRS. FLANAGAN Happiness. Feckin' A.

MR. O'FLANAGAN Well sure ye're movin' to the world capital o' happiness, for the payple of Ireland are in a state of hysterical felicitation twenty-four hours a day. They're mad with happiness, I tell ye, they're positively maaaaad with it.

JASIU It wouldn't be the blarney you're after handing me?

ALL THE FLANAGANS Nivver. Nivver. Nivver. Nivver.

MR. O'FLANAGAN Why the payple of Ireland are so insane with cheer, laughin' and jokin' and sighin' with peace all the time, there's actually asylums for the criminally content! And why?

MISS MACFLANAGAN Because ye'll find no accordions in the old country.

MRS. FLANAGAN No, nor no sausages neither.

MR. O'FLANAGAN No *Polish people,* if ye ken what I mean.

MISS MACFLANAGAN Ye can pronounce the name of every darlin' lad and lassie.

MRS. FLANAGAN Our beer has nivver an egg nor salt, nor our soups contain no blood o' the duck.

MR. O'FLANAGAN   There's no steel mills, only green hills and blue sky and the softest turf in creation. (*Produces a square foot of grassy turf*)   Just feel that turf.

JASIU   Amazing!

MRS. FLANAGAN   How would ye like to fook on that?

JASIU   Well, I'm ready. What's the price on a one-way ticket?

MR. O'FLANAGAN   Just a moment. Just a moment, now. You see, sar, the cost of a ticket—in particular, a *one-way* ticket—to the blessed isle, fluctuates, by order of the Vatican, depending on sartain sarrcumstances.

JASIU   What sarta sarcumstances?

MR. O'FLANAGAN   Well, sar. Ye say ye're goin' for happiness. Now, the Flanagan clan bein' by tradition a particularly happy one, ye force me to an embarrassing question before I print yer ticket. And I'm tinkin' of this here young widow-to-be's future. Mr. Flanagan—are ye a true Flanagan, or are ye a fake Flanagan, fraudulently flyin' the Flanagan flag?

JASIU   No. Listen. The flag I fly is fully the finest Flanagan. . . flannel . . . forsooth . . .

MR. O'FLANAGAN   Ah-ha. Ah-ha. Well, just to certify that your flannel is fully Flanagan, we have an optional Saint Shamus Day quiz for ye. Do not be ashamed if ye don't want to take the optional quiz. Do ye want to take the . . . ?

JASIU   I do. I do. I do.

MR. O'FLANAGAN   So. Question number one, sar, for a two-thousand-dollar ticket: Are ye sometimes overcome by irrational bouts of optimism and happiness and hope?

JASIU   Aye, sir, that I am.

MR. O'FLANAGAN   Correct! And now for the eight-thousand-dollar ticket.

MISS MACFLANAGAN   Bein' Irish have ye heard . . . the Irish Triangle?

JASIU   The Irish Triangle . . .

MR. O'FLANAGAN   Tink hard, now. The Irish Triangle. Maybe you're doin' something personal in the bathroom and suddenly ye hear . . . (*We hear a triangle tinkling.*) . . . the Irish Triangle. And abruptly ye're paralyzed by happiness, ye're seized by a senseless joy, and ye break into an Irish reel?

JASIU   Twenty times a day!

MR. O'FLANAGAN   Twenty times a day, says he!
(*Jubilation*)   And finally, sar, the final question. Mrs. F?

MRS. FLANAGAN   Can ye sing. . . "Danny Boy"?

JASIU (*Sings*)   "Oh Danny Boy . . ."

JASIU & MISS MACFLANAGAN   ". . . the pipes, the pipes are callin'. . ."

ALL THE FLANAGANS (*Very fast, to get it over with*)   ". . . fromglentoglenanddownthemountainside."

MRS. FLANAGAN   Whoo!

MISS MACFLANAGAN   Jaysus be praised!

MRS. FLANAGAN   He's the real feckin' thing!

MR. O'FLANAGAN   Congratulations, Mr. Flanagan, ye've won a one-way ticket to Ireland for only *twenty-eight thousand dollars*!

More jubilation.

JASIU Here's my credit card.

Total jubilation.

MR. O'FLANAGAN And here's yer ticket. (*He hands Jasiu a ticket.*) Miss Shishlayvitch!

MISS MACFLANAGAN Yes, Mr. Pshibillchik!

JASIU Pshibillchik . . . ?

MRS. FLANAGAN (*Clears her throat loudly to warn them*)

MISS MACFLANAGAN Did I say Pshibillchik? I mean—yes, Mr. O'Flanagan.

MR. O'FLANAGAN Will ye see the gentleman out. And top o' the mornin' to ye, sir!

JASIU Top o' the mornin' . . .

MRS. FLANAGAN Top o' the mornin', Mr. Flanagan!

JASIU Top o' the mornin' to you, Mrs. Flanagan . . .

MR. O'FLANAGAN And a hearty top o' the mornin' to us all!

Mr. O'Flanagan and Mrs. Flanagan exit.

MISS MACFLANAGAN We three here are in exile from all the old country's happiness. But ye shall have it all. That ye may nivver forget me, here's a triangle to wear about your neck. And when ye want to tink of me, just tinkle. (*Gives him a triangle.*) God bless and speed you on your happy way, Black Jack Flanagan. And as soon as the bloated stinkin' corpse of Michael MacMcFlanagan washes up I'll be a-waitin' for you with arms wide open on MacFishbellybelly Strand. And together for life we'll do the Irish reel.

Miss MacFlanagan exits.

JASIU Happiness . . . !

Thunder and lightning as THADDEUS KOSCIUSZKO *appears, in eighteenth-century wig and breeches.*

SCENE THREE

KOSCIUSZKO (*Echo effect*) *Jan Bogdan Sodwoofski*! Do you know who I am?

JASIU You couldn't be . . . You're not telling me . . . Are you Thaddeus Kosciuszko?

KOSCIUSZKO I am Tadeusz Andrzej Bonawentura Kosciuszko! (*"Tah-DAY-oosh AHN-jay Bawn-ah-ven-TOO-rah Kawsh-CHOOSH-kaw"*) Brigadier general in the American Revolution. Defender of West Point. Polish patriot and hero. Dead since 1817. What have *you* been doing lately?

JASIU Well, I wrote a highly acclaimed novel . . .

Lightning and thunder.

KOSCIUSZKO Tell me, O Sodwoofski: Why are you moving to Ireland?

JASIU Listen, I don't have to explain myself to you.

KOSCIUSZKO You have to explain yourself to somebody. I ask you this, O Mr. so-called Sadler: a not-so-optional quiz. Do you want to take the not-so-optional quiz?

JASIU Not really.

KOSCIUSZKO *What is Poland?* (*Jasiu says nothing.*) You say nothing. I say, Poland is a great mystery!

JASIU Poland is a lot of things, but it's not . . .

KOSCIUSZKO   *A great mystery!* In the year 1795, Poland is
under attack. The Russians hold that—(*Points off stage
left*)   The Prussians hold that—(*Points off right*)   The
Austrians, that. The Lithuanians—a loud people—hold that.
(*Up left*)   And the Swedes—(*Up right*)   all that. Poland is
reduced to one single handful of earth that they battle
over. This handful. (*He takes out a handful of dirt.*)   This
fistful of dirt is all that is left of Poland. So I ask you, what
is Poland that all the nations of Europe want her? That
even Napoleon desires her? What do these peoples lack
which only Poland can give them? Do you not see?
Poland must be golden. Every grain of Polish soil must be
more precious than diamonds! More fertile than woman!
She is the Helen of Troy, the Cleopatra among the
peoples of the world, that all these great nations desire her.
Teutonic barbarians! Poland is greater than you all! You will
die—but Poland can never die! (*Pause. He tosses Jasiu the
handful of dirt.*)   Think about it. *Do widzenia!*

Kosciuszko disappears. Jasiu tosses away the dirt.

Scene Four

*Jasiu's place. A particularly dissonant string quartet, something like
Bartok's third, plays as background. Jasiu tapes boxes shut as Rachel
watches.*

RACHEL   So you're running away.

JASIU   I'm not running away. I'm moving away.

RACHEL   You're packing like a man being pursued.

JASIU   I am pursued. "For at my back I always hear . . ."

RACHEL   I always hear . . . something . . . something . . .

JASIU "Time's wingèd chariot hurrying near."

RACHEL Shakespeare.

JASIU No.

RACHEL Keats.

JASIU No.

RACHEL Lucille Ball? It's something very famous, right?

JASIU What does it matter what it is.

RACHEL I'm sorry.

JASIU Rachel, look. You've got nothing to apologize for. Neither of us has anything to apologize for.

RACHEL *You* do. For playing this wretched noise when I'm trying to say good-bye to you.

JASIU Sorry.

She turns off the Bartok.

RACHEL Do they even allow Bartok into Ireland? If they frisk you at the airport and find Bartok they'll send you home.

JASIU Let 'em try.

RACHEL I hope they do send you home.

JASIU Poland disappeared. I can too. Seven-ten tomorrow night, I happily vanish.

RACHEL Have we not been pretty damn spectacular?

JASIU Well . . . "Everything gets spoiled."

RACHEL I'm sorry I couldn't change your mind about that. What has spoiled *us*? Nothing.

Polish Joke

JASIU I guess I have.

RACHEL I'm sorry I let that happen.

JASIU It wasn't *you*.

RACHEL Then I'm sorry to be driving you away.

JASIU Will you stop apologizing?

RACHEL I'm sorry we don't fit. I'm sorry I don't turn you on.

JASIU As if anything could.

RACHEL I'm sorry I don't look good in red and white.

JASIU Forget that. Just . . .

RACHEL They're not my colors. And I'm sorry I don't know Shakespeare and Beethoven and . . . Latin . . . and . . .

JASIU And all the other things that bore the *shite* out of people these days. It's a lonely country for anybody in the Shakespeare and Beethoven societies. Anyway, I'm not moving because of you. If I stay any longer on this side of the world, if I *fail* any longer on this side of the world . . .

RACHEL You haven't failed. You're just incredibly . . .

JASIU Polish.

RACHEL Unlucky.

JASIU Call it unlucky. Call it fate.

RACHEL You really do believe in fate.

JASIU I'm fated to believe in fate. To paraphrase an obscure Roman poet.

RACHEL   Maybe if you didn't read obscure Roman poets all day, you'd feel better about life. And stay over here.

JASIU   And do what? And become what? I was brought up to be a polite peasant, pulling my forelock and bowing. Yes sir. No ma'am. Please, take my seat. Where's that kind of behavior going to get you in the pushy republic of America? Even if you're not Polish.

RACHEL   What if my father called me up and said, Honey, I've got news, you're Polish. Do you really think anything would change?

JASIU   Are you ever overwhelmed by a tragic feeling of discouragement, disappointment, and despair?

RACHEL   No.

JASIU   You're not Polish. Rejoice. I can't.

RACHEL   And *"Flanagan"*?

JASIU   Yes. Why not.

RACHEL   "John Flanagan"?

JASIU   There's nothing wrong with "Flanagan."

RACHEL   How many times are you going to change your name? Who *are* you? I love you, Jack. Does that count for nothing?

JASIU   This was inevitable.

RACHEL   Right.

JASIU   We were never going to work out.

RACHEL   Right.

BOTH   *Everything gets spoiled.*

RACHEL   I wish human beings were equipped with mental *delete* buttons, so we could wipe out the things our mothers tell us. And stupid ideas like fate.

JASIU   *Fate* is the least of my stupid ideas.

RACHEL   If there is such a thing as fate, running away to Ireland won't help anything.

JASIU   Of course it won't. But I can make a show of it, can't I? I can *try* to be happy, can't I?

RACHEL   What'll you do over there?

JASIU   I don't know. Listen to Bartok. Miss you. Or, if you're so determined . . .

RACHEL   No, Jack.

JASIU   Come with me. Come along.

RACHEL   I can't. I'm not Irish, like you are.

JASIU   Okay. Okay.

RACHEL   Good-bye, Jack.

Rachel exits.

JASIU (*A sudden pain in his foot*)   Ow!

SCENE FIVE

A doctor's office, with examining table. DOCTOR *enters.*

DOCTOR   Mr. Finnegan?

JASIU (*Hopping on one leg*)   Ow! Ow! Ow! Ow!

DOCTOR   John Finnegan?

JASIU *FLANAGAN.* John *FLANAGAN.*

DOCTOR Sorry. I've looked at your X-rays, Mr. Flanagan. Quite an amazing case.

JASIU This can't be happening. I'm moving to Ireland today, at seven-ten tonight.

DOCTOR You won't be moving far on that. You've broken your footbone.

JASIU My what?

DOCTOR Your footbone. And you've broken it *all the way up.* Nurse!

NURSE *enters.*

NURSE Yes, Doctor.

DOCTOR Come in, please. I'd like you to observe this. Do you have the instruments?

NURSE Right here, Doctor.

DOCTOR Scalpel!

NURSE Scalpel!

Apparently they just like to say these words, since the Nurse hands him nothing.

JASIU But I didn't do anything! I spent the day packing. I went to bed perfectly fine.

DOCTOR & NURSE Mmm-hmm.

JASIU Nothing wrong, no pain.

DOCTOR & NURSE Mmm-hmm.

JASIU I woke up and I fell over; I couldn't walk.

DOCTOR Well it's not surprising. You'd broken your footbone.

JASIU In my sleep?

DOCTOR Apparently. Clamp!

NURSE Clamp!

DOCTOR Have you been doing a lot of running?

JASIU No.

DOCTOR Or *running away*?

JASIU No.

DOCTOR Retractor!

NURSE Retractor!

DOCTOR Were you dreaming last night?

JASIU Does it really matter?

DOCTOR Maybe you had some very strenuous or erotic dream. Maybe a woman was tying your footbone to a bedpost.

JASIU No. No. No.

DOCTOR I'm just trying to find out what we've got here, Mr. um . . .

JASIU *Flanagan.*

DOCTOR Flanagan. Tell me, sir, what kind of music do you listen to?

JASIU I don't know. Bartok. Shostakovich.

DOCTOR Bartok and Shostakovich!

NURSE Bartok and Shostakovich!

DOCTOR Mmm–hmm.

JASIU So I listen to Bartok and Shostakovich!

DOCTOR Suture!

NURSE Suture!

DOCTOR Suit yourself, but that's awfully heavy music for a man with a foot like yours.

JASIU I'm leaving. (*Stopped by pain*) Ow!

DOCTOR White cane!

NURSE White cane!

JASIU I'm not *blind,* for God's sake.

DOCTOR Not to our knowledge. Other cane!

NURSE Other cane!

JASIU NO!

DOCTOR Novocaine!

NURSE Novocaine!

DOCTOR You know, you may have been crippled as a child. One isn't supposed to use the word *crippled* anymore. (*Whispers*) *Bad connotations. Lowers self-esteem.* But now that you're crippled, what's the difference? When you were young, did you ever play doctor, maybe with a sibling or a neighbor?

JASIU So what if I did?

DOCTOR Maybe you broke your footbone so we could look at your genitals. Am I right, Nurse?

NURSE   You're right, Doctor.

DOCTOR   Are you married?

NURSE   Five times.

DOCTOR   I was speaking to Mr. what's-his-name. Are you married?

JASIU   No.

DOCTOR   Are you straight?

JASIU   Yes.

DOCTOR   Are you getting laid?

JASIU   It's none of your business.

DOCTOR   Do you want to show me your genitals?

JASIU   No!

DOCTOR   Can I show you *my* genitals?

JASIU   *No!*

DOCTOR   This kind of fracture frequently occurs with age, you know.

JASIU   I'm not that old.

DOCTOR   Who knows when death will come? This could be your last day on earth. You could kick off like that. Am I right, Nurse?

NURSE   You're right, Doctor.

DOCTOR   Looking at your chart, there is one other possible explanation for your condition, Mr., um, John. I don't quite know how to tell you this. Would you read the eye chart, please?

Nurse unveils an eye chart.

JASIU "P."

DOCTOR Next line.

JASIU "O. L."

DOCTOR Good. Next line.

JASIU "A. N. D."

DOCTOR Excellent. (*Nurse opens her uniform to reveal a red-and-white teddy.*) On this satin teddy, what color do you see on the tits?

JASIU Red.

DOCTOR And on the hips?

JASIU White.

DOCTOR Good. Do these colors give you an erection? What some doctors would call a "hard-on"? You're shivering.

JASIU I'm not shivering.

DOCTOR You're sweating.

JASIU I'm not sweating.

DOCTOR Do you ever get a ringing in your ears? Sounds something like this?

Nurse produces a large gong and bangs it. Jasiu reacts with a groan.

DOCTOR Mmm-hmm. Mmm-hmm. Well, sir, comparing you and your X-rays, here's my diagnosis: You could be Polish. Are you Polish? I may as well tell you I'm half Polish myself. On my left side. My mother's side.

JASIU Well, you're a half-assed doctor, whatever your ethnic background.

DOCTOR You know this isn't the first time I've heard that.

JASIU Why am I not surprised?

DOCTOR *Are* you Polish, sir?

JASIU All right, all right! I'm Polish!

DOCTOR Well, there! Don't you feel better already?

JASIU Better?

DOCTOR This explains everything! You've had an absurd accident. There's really only one rational explanation. Nurse?

NURSE Polish.

DOCTOR You're Polish! For example, look at *me. Look! At! Me! (Jasiu does so.)*   For years I wondered why I was such a half-assed doctor. I killed several patients on the operating table. Two on a miniature golf course. I sliced it too hard. As a human being, I was a goof. A clown. A fuckup. A shmo.

NURSE It's true.

DOCTOR I picked this nostril constantly. I was impotent.

NURSE It's true.

DOCTOR I thought it was me. Then my half-sister half-hinted I was half Polish. It's amazing the instant relief I felt. I wasn't hexed, or cursed, or doomed, or inept, or even particularly stupid. I was just Polish. Well, half Polish. So I semiretired. Anyway, I recommend being Polish, or claiming to be Polish, to just about every troubled person I know.

JASIU Claiming to be Polish?

DOCTOR Don't you see the beauty of it? Your sickness is your cure! Nurse?

NURSE It's true, Mr. Flanagan. For example, look at *me*. *LOOK! AT! ME!* (*Jasiu does so.*)   I used to blame myself for four failed marriages and my problems with alcohol and crack cocaine. Then my tarot card reader told me I was Polish. Now my fifth marriage is falling apart and I'm still on crack but at least I know *why*. Now I'm feeling good about myself and my self-esteem is high. All thanks to Poland!

DOCTOR Maybe you should ask Nurse to dinner.

JASIU *I don't want to ask Nurse to dinner.*

DOCTOR You're shivering.

JASIU I'm not shivering.

DOCTOR Did you hear about the Polack who studied five days for his urine test? And *still* got an F?

JASIU Will you just tell me what I can do about my footbone?

DOCTOR Frankly, nothing. If I were you, I'd go someplace for half a year and wear a half-cast 50 percent of the time. Someplace where there's nothing to see and nothing to do, no distractions, some bare flat gloomy country where you'll be up against unornamented existence, the stark and scary facts of reality. Maybe . . .

JASIU Poland?

DOCTOR Maybe Poland. Or, if you're half Polish, maybe . . .

JASIU Half-Poland?

DOCTOR Maybe half-Poland. Try the city of Woodge.

JASIU Why is the universe always pushing me toward Poland?

NURSE We're in exile from Poland.

DOCTOR Or, half of Poland.

NURSE But you'll get to have it all.

DOCTOR Do you know the name of the Polish airline?

JASIU Lot.

DOCTOR Need I say more? (*Hops onto the table and the Nurse pushes him out.*) Table!

NURSE Table!

DOCTOR Doorway!

NURSE Doorway!

DOCTOR Knockers!

NURSE Knockers!

Nurse and Doctor exit.

JASIU Well, I'm not going to Poland. I'm moving to Ireland. And you're not going to stop me! I've got my ticket!

SCENE SIX

Airplane. Jasiu takes a seat and reads the Irish Times.

STEWARDESS'S VOICE (*Irish brogue, over loudspeaker*) Ladies and gentlemen, good morning and welcome to Aer Lingus flight 711 to Dublin. My name is Miss O'MacO'McFlanagan. I'll be your cabin attendant today. And what a fine and lovely and grand and blessed day it is, too. Why sure the silver-lined clouds are as poofy as the buttocks on the pigs in County Cork. Now sit back, relax, and enjoy your flight to the Emerald Isle.

Ladislaw enters, still in miner's hat and overalls, still with toilet plunger.

LADISLAW (*Singing*) "Ohhhh see can yow sigh . . . by down's eerily liggit . . ." (*He sits down next to Jasiu.*) We are there now? This is Warsaw? Where is this?

JASIU Warsaw?

LADISLAW No. Is ocean. (*Calls back to another seat*) Zawsha! We are over ocean! No Poland yet! (*To Jasiu*) *Dzień dobry.*

JASIU Hello.

LADISLAW *Jak się masz.*

JASIU Mm-hmm.

LADISLAW I am Ladislaw Sadlowski. My family is coming from America.

JASIU Obviously.

LADISLAW We are moving back to Poland. America is beautiful. America is wonderful. But America is not Poland.

JASIU That's what you think.

LADISLAW (*Offering one*) You want blood sausage?

JASIU No, thanks. So you're connecting to Warsaw from Dublin . . . ?

LADISLAW No, we are flying to Warsaw now! On this plane!

JASIU I don't believe this flight goes to Poland.

LADISLAW (*Shows ticket*)   Oh, yes. Lot Polish Airlines flight 666. Warsaw.

JASIU   This is Aer Lingus you're on.

LADISLAW   No.

JASIU   Flight 711. To Ireland.

LADISLAW   *Okholera!* (*Calls*)   Zawsha! This is not plane to Warsaw! This is Air Quinnilinguis, to Iceland! Now we have to fly back to America to fly to Poland!

STEWARDESS'S VOICE   Ladies and gentlemen, Miss O'MacO'McFlanagan again. We've just had some news from the cockpit. Due to weather conditions over Ireland, our flight today has been diverted to Warsaw, Poland.

JASIU   No. No . . . !

STEWARDESS'S VOICE   With connections to Woodge.

JASIU (*Trying to climb out of his seat*)   No! Stewardess! Stewardess!

STEWARDESS'S VOICE   And stay in yer feckin' seat until the BLOODY LIGHT IS OFF!

JASIU   Stop this plane! I will not go to Poland!

STEWARDESS'S VOICE   Top o' the mornin' to ye!

SCENE SEVEN

Warsaw. A "LOT" airport counter. OLGA enters through a door marked "NO EXIT." She wears a red-and-white uniform.

JASIU   Damn it. Damn it. Damn it. Damn it.

OLGA   *Dzień dobry.* Can I help you?

JASIU   Magda?!

OLGA   Olga.

JASIU   Sorry.

OLGA   Olga Welma Wanda Josefina Wilkomirska. (*"OL-gah VEL-mah VON-dah Yaw-zeh-FEE-nah Veel-ko-MEER-skah"*)   Velcome to Varsaw.

JASIU   May I call you Olga?

OLGA   No.

JASIU   Listen, Ms. Wilkomirska, I'm supposed to be in Ireland right now.

OLGA   Yes? Why?

JASIU   Because it's my home.

OLGA   You live in Ireland?

JASIU   No, I'm happily moving to Ireland.

OLGA   So, you are Irish?

JASIU   It doesn't matter if I'm Irish. You don't have to be Irish to live in Ireland.

OLGA   So, you are not Irish.

JASIU   What I am, is I'm due to meet somebody on MacFishbellybelly Strand, and what is Lot Airlines going to do about it?

OLGA   Lot flies you to Ireland. (*Checks schedule*)   Next Wednesday. Maybe.

JASIU   You're not serious.

OLGA   I am serious person.

JASIU I'm not staying in Poland till next Wednesday. I'm not staying here till *tomorrow*.

OLGA Something is wrong with Poland?

JASIU Okay, you won't help me. May I speak to your superior?

OLGA I am my superior.

JASIU Where's the train station?

OLGA There are no trains to Ireland. It is completely surrounded by water.

JASIU All right, then. I'll walk. (*Starts away*) Ow! Ow!

OLGA Something is wrong with foot?

JASIU Yes, something is wrong with foot!

OLGA Footbone is broken?

JASIU What's it to you?

OLGA You break this footbone in your sleep?

JASIU How did you know that?

OLGA I see this all the time. I break both my feet, twice, all the way up. Too many dreams.

JASIU Look, Miss Wilkormirska, will you help me out as a fellow countryman?

OLGA You are from this country?

JASIU Metaphorically.

OLGA Poland is metaphor?

JASIU Actually—I mean, originally—actually, I'm Polish myself.

OLGA   You? Polish yourself? No.

JASIU   Yes.

OLGA   No, you are not Polish.

JASIU   I'm of Polish descent.

OLGA   *John Flanagan?*

JASIU   Jan Bogdan Sodwoofski.

OLGA   Hmp.

JASIU   Call me Jasiu.

OLGA   I can see you are not Polish.

JASIU   Well, I know I'm Polish.

OLGA   No. You don't know this.

JASIU   What, I've been misinformed all these years?

OLGA   Who tells you you are Polish?

JASIU   My parents.

OLGA   They are misinformed.

JASIU   "Sodwoofski" isn't Polish?

OLGA   It is if you are Polish.

JASIU   Okay . . .

OLGA   Why is it so important if you are Polish? Who cares?

JASIU   Look, everybody in my family back to the Pleistocene was Polish. That's not Polish?

OLGA   I am from Poland, you are in Poland, you think I don't recognize Polish person?

JASIU Okay. Okay. Okay. I'm not Polish. Will you help me if I'm not Polish?

OLGA Maybe you are Jewish.

JASIU I'm not Jewish.

OLGA You're ashamed of being Jewish?

JASIU No, and I'm not ashamed of not being Jewish either.

OLGA You are all right? You are shivering.

JASIU I'm not shivering.

OLGA You are sweating.

JASIU I'm fine. I'm fine.

OLGA Maybe this is my red–and–white uniform.

JASIU How do you know that?

OLGA Polish people know things other people do not know. As your Shakespeare says, "In nature's infinite book of secrecy, I can read a little."

JASIU Shakespeare . . .

OLGA I am reading *Hamlet,* maybe, every week. I am president of Polish Shakespeare Society.

JASIU Ms. Wilkomirska, does life sometimes seem totally meaningless to you?

OLGA Every day.

JASIU Are you ever overcome by a tragic feeling of disappointment and discouragement?

OLGA Of course.

JASIU Total despair?

OLGA All the time.

JASIU Well so am I!

OLGA What are you saying? This is Polish gloom? No! Everybody has this gloom.

JASIU Not everybody has this gloom. You and I do. And I bet things tend not to work out for you, don't they?

OLGA Of course not. Everything gets spoiled. Is human condition.

JASIU Hanging sausages in the living room? That's the human condition?

OLGA Yes.

JASIU Learning to polka?

OLGA Yes.

JASIU Playing Saint Mary Magdalene in the Saint Casimir Easter pageant? That's the human condition?

OLGA Yes.

JASIU Playing Polish army hospital? Years of obsession about women dressed like the Polish flag? Duck blood soup? That's not Polish, that's just the human condition?

OLGA Yes.

JASIU Well it's certainly been *my* condition. I make myself into somebody else—and it's *the wrong person!* I change my name and people *still* can't get it right! How's that for a Polack thing to do? I learn Shakespeare, Beethoven, Bartok. Only to see that lot get flushed down the multicultural toilet because they're men or they're dead or they're not as relevant as whatever narcotic garbage is on the tube this week. How's that for a Polack thing to do? And you're going to tell me I've been through all this—*for nothing*? If I'm not Polish, what the hell am I, Ms. Wilkomirska? Who am I?

OLGA Maybe you are simply a fool. Do you love Poland?

JASIU No.

OLGA Then you are not Polish. The country you love, the country you defend, that is your country. But you—I can see it—you hate Poland. You are ashamed of Poland. You are ashamed to think you're Polish. And you tell me you are Polish? Fuck you. Live here, then tell me you are Polish. You read Shakespeare. Do you read our poets? Kochanowski? Szymborska? Milosz? Herbert? Mickiewicz? You listen to Bartok and Beethoven, but do you listen to Penderecki, Lutoslawski, Gorecki, Szymanowski? Then you are not Polish. Did you want to come here? No, you are fighting to go away. So go. Please. Poland has been the garbage can of Europe for centuries. The country is backward, the people have little. *This* is why you are ashamed. Because Poland and the Polish people are not successful, and important. And prosperous. Because we are not Americans. The Nazis killed three million Poles. Not only the Polish Jews, three million *Poles*. Catholics. Lutherans. Exterminated. Who says *this*? Who makes movies about *this*? You don't want to be Polish? Don't want to be. Go to Ireland. Be American. *Jasiu*. But get out of the country that I love. That I live in every day, and that I *love*.

Olga exits.

JASIU (*He speaks to us.*)   What else could I do? I married her. You might say I woke up from the dream I'd been having for so many years. Or moved on to a different dream . . .

Like a sleepwalker who wakes in a panic, thinking he's walking on the edge of a roof, about to fall—and finds himself on flat land, with a woman touching his arm and saying, Honey, come to bed. Honey, come to bed . . .

SCENE EIGHT

The driveway again, with two lawn chairs. Roman enters, carrying two beer steins.

ROMAN I brung you a snifter, Jasiu.

JASIU Thanks, Uncle Roman.

ROMAN Pull up a lawn chair.

JASIU The same old lawn chairs.

ROMAN Nah, it's new lawn chairs, they just look the same. (*They sit.*) So, Jasiu. You come back to the Bush.

JASIU Just for a few days.

ROMAN Did you go to the cemetery?

JASIU I did.

ROMAN Did you put some flowers on your mother's and father's graves?

JASIU I did.

ROMAN The whole family's there now, practically. My Helen is there.

JASIU You're not there.

ROMAN Not yet. The doctors give me three to six months. You heard about that.

JASIU   Yes I did.

ROMAN   Sure, that's why you're sitting here right now. The doctors wanted me to do chemo, I says no. God wants me to die, I got nothing to be afraid of.

JASIU   There aren't too many people who'd feel that way, Uncle Roman.

ROMAN   You know what's the only thing I'm gonna miss? The only thing I'm gonna miss is the smell of women. Oh Jeezu, I love the smell of women. You know, Jasiu, you're just like you were as a little boy.

JASIU   I am?

ROMAN   Whoa, yeah.

JASIU   What was I like as a little boy?

ROMAN   Just like you are now. Staring at me like that.

JASIU   Maybe I'm the same, but the Bush sure has changed.

ROMAN   Yeah, the steel mill's closed down fifteen years now. At the parish there's maybe twenty Polish families. I got a Jamaican woman from down the block comes and makes my food. I'm eating curried goat. You ever had curried goat, Jasiu?

JASIU   No.

ROMAN   Oh, Jesus, it's wonderful. I woulda been eating goat all my life if I'da known. You just gotta start with the right goat.

JASIU   Sure, sure.

ROMAN   My Jamaican lady, she says all the curry in the world won't save a bad goat.

JASIU I bet.

ROMAN What a world.

JASIU I wonder what ever happened to Magda.

ROMAN Magda Kotchmarek . . . She's got a Fortune 500 company and lives in Tucson. And I bet she's still wearin' that goddamn rhinestone tiara. Howbout you, Jasiu? You like living in Poland?

JASIU Yes I do.

ROMAN I always meant to get over to the old country. Is it beauty-ful?

JASIU Is Poland beautiful . . . I don't know . . . It's a place that really forces you to look at it. (*Roman has a hard coughing fit.*) Anyway, it's home now.

ROMAN You got a family now.

JASIU Yep. Olga and the twins. Velma and Vanda.

ROMAN Took you a while.

JASIU Yeah, well. Life locked my family in a car, it took me thirty years to get them out.

ROMAN And tell me. Are you happy, my godson? You got anything to say to me, you better say it now, you ain't gonna get another chance. Are you happy?

JASIU Well . . . I guess I'm still learning how to be.

ROMAN Do you serve God?

JASIU I don't think I believe in God anymore.

ROMAN Do you serve him anyway?

JASIU I try.

ROMAN Then you got nothing to worry about. Nothing can touch you. Death cannot touch you.

JASIU The Gong still rings sometimes. But not like it used to.

ROMAN The Gong . . .

JASIU You were a huge influence on me, Uncle Roman.

ROMAN Who.

JASIU You. A huge influence.

ROMAN I never saw that much a you.

JASIU Sundays for sausage.

ROMAN Sure, sausages, once in a while.

JASIU You changed my life.

ROMAN You know, Jasiu, one time a long time ago I told you something that was wrong. I told you one time that people were different. But you know what? People are not different. People are exactly the same.

JASIU Well, maybe not exactly the same . . .

ROMAN Yeah, all people are exactly the same.

JASIU Except Lithuanians, who are loud.

ROMAN Everybody's loud sometimes. You remember in the Gospel, Jesus says the master hired workers for the vineyard, some worked one hour and some worked six hours and some worked nine hours, but they all got paid the same ting? They all got paid one drachma.

JASIU The ones who worked nine hours were probably Polish.

ROMAN It don't matter what the were, Jasiu. They all got their drachma. I got my drachma. You got your drachma. My Jamaican goat-maker, she's got a drachma. Alla those people got their drachmas. We're all the same.

JASIU Now you tell me.

ROMAN What the hell did I know? I'm a Polack.

JASIU You knew a lot.

ROMAN You spend your drachma well. (*Toasting: "Nahz DRAWV-yeh", "to your health"*) *Na zdrowie.*

JASIU *Na zdrowie.*

They clink steins.

ROMAN Drink, Jasiu. Drink.

JASIU Do you mind if I have one without an egg?

ROMAN The beer wouldn't taste right without an egg.

JASIU At least without the salt?

ROMAN The egg don't taste right without salt. Besides, the egg is for life, the salt is for tears.

JASIU I never knew that.

ROMAN Yeah. Egg for life, salt for tears.

JASIU What does the beer stand for?

ROMAN The beer stands for beer.

JASIU You know, Uncle Roman, I've never found anybody in all of Poland who drinks beer with an egg and salt.

ROMAN No.

JASIU Yes.

ROMAN   You're kidding. Not even in Woodge?

JASIU   Not even in the great city of Woodge.

ROMAN   What the hell have I been drinking this shit for all
my life?

JASIU   Maybe it's a local custom.

ROMAN   Maybe it's a *local custom*. You go first. (*Jasiu
drinks.*)   And how is that Polish beer, Jasiu?

JASIU   Good. The beer is good, Uncle Roman. It's very, very
good.

ROMAN   Good. *Now let the great ceremony begin!* (*Small
pause*)   Did you hear the one about the Polish brain
surgeon?

JASIU (*Laughing*)   Okay. Tell me.

ROMAN   This guy walks into a doctor's office, the doctor says,
Bend over . . .

The lights have faded on them.

END OF PLAY

ANCIENT HISTORY

This one-act version of *Ancient History* was produced by Primary Stages (Casey Childs, artistic director) in New York City, in June 1996. The director was John Rando; the set designer, Loren Sherman; the costume designer, Rodney Munoz; the lighting designer, Deborah Constantine; the sound designer, Jim Van Bergen; and the stage manager, Christine Catti. The cast was as follows:

RUTH	Vivienne Benesch
JACK	Michael Rupert

An earlier, two-act version of the play was also produced at Primary Stages, with Beth McDonald and Christopher Wells in the two roles, directed by Jason McConnell Buzas.

The characters: RUTH *and* JACK, *an attractive couple in their thirties.*

The setting: An apartment. A bed. A fireplace with a mirror over it. A telephone. A door to the outside. A door to a bathroom. A doorway to a kitchen. Scattered about the room, a pair of men's pants, a shirt, socks, and shoes. A blue dress hangs in the bathroom doorway.

In the dark, a phone rings, loudly, once—the bell of an old ringer-type telephone, echoing into silence. Then we hear "Oui, c'est elle, c'est la déesse" from Bizet's Pearl Fishers *as lights come up on Ruth and Jack dancing slowly in each other's arms. They are barefoot, in robes.*

They dip together. A phone rings, once. They freeze in position. Lights fade a little, then rise back as Jack and Ruth start dancing again, as the music goes back a few bars and goes on.

RUTH   Paradise.

JACK   Absolutely.

RUTH   Paradise.

JACK   But absolutely.—*Dip.* (*They dip.*)

RUTH   Now this is what I call *shayn.*

JACK   Me too. What's a "*shayn*"?

RUTH   *Shayn* is an ancient Yiddish word, for "pretty damn nifty."

JACK   Ah-ha. "*Shayn!* Come back!"

RUTH   *Dip.* Is this a couple, or what?

JACK   Looks like a couple to me.

RUTH   Now what do you say we never, ever stop.

A phone rings, loudly, once. They stop dancing. The music goes back a few bars and they resume.

JACK   "*Shayn!* Come back!"

103

RUTH So are we setting up for this party, or are we dancing?

JACK We're dancing. Obviously.

RUTH Oh, right. So we are.

JACK And we're dancing to *The Pearl Fishers,* which nobody else in the world can dance to.

RUTH & JACK *Dip.*

RUTH Is this a couple, or what?

JACK Tall and thin and funny. Looks like a couple to me.

RUTH Can you imagine what the world would be like if everybody lived like this?

JACK It'd be utopia.

RUTH Earthly paradise.

JACK Absolutely.

RUTH There'd be no war.

JACK No strife.

RUTH No hunger.

JACK No hatred.

RUTH No polyester.

JACK And *no parents.* (*The phone rings loudly, once. Then they continue dancing as before.*) Dip.

RUTH Dip.

JACK Can you imagine what the world would be like if everybody lived like this?

RUTH It'd be paradise.

JACK   Absolutely.

RUTH   No war. No . . .

JACK   Strife. No . . .

RUTH   Varicose veins.

JACK   Sorry, Pinky. Those ugly blue veins are part of nature's grand design.

RUTH   Would you still dance with me if I had varicose veins?

JACK   Of course not.

RUTH   Would it be all over?

JACK   It would be *all over.*

RUTH   You're not supposed to say things like that on my *birthday.*

JACK   (*An old routine between them*)   What? I'm *not?*

RUTH & JACK (*Together*)   *Uh-oh!*

They dip. Phone rings. The music fades out.

JACK   Sorry, Ginger. That was the dip that broke the camel's back. (*He shuffles over and drops onto the bed.*)

RUTH   Hey, hey, hey. Don't tell me this dance is over already?

JACK   I'm depleted from sex. See? No pleats. "Depleted"— "no pleats"?

RUTH   Oh, what a clever child it is. But speaking of *birthdays* . . .

JACK   Birthdays, birthdays . . . ? Did I ever tell you I spent my twenty-first birthday making love in a tree?

RUTH   Oh, I'd say about twenty times.

JACK   Do I repeat myself? Very well then, I repeat myself.

RUTH   Didn't somebody say, "Hell is other people"—?

JACK   J. P. Sartre, who actually said, "*Hotel* is other people."

RUTH   Hell isn't other people. It's other people telling the same story for the twentieth time.

JACK   And you know what *that* is, don't you?

RUTH   What . . .

JACK & RUTH (*Together*)   *Marriage.*

RUTH   Oh, good. We are onto marriage and ready for blastoff.

JACK   It's in the dictionary. "Marriage. Archaic noun. Two people telling each other the same story for the twentieth time."

RUTH   Mm-hmm.

JACK   Did I ever tell you I spent my twenty-first birthday making love in a tree?

RUTH   It wasn't the horrid ex-wife up that tree, was it?

JACK   It was the horrid ex-wife. Nibbling rodents.

RUTH   Was horrid ex-wife as good-looking as me?

JACK   Never.

RUTH   That's all right, then. But speaking of *birthdays* . . .

JACK   Birthdays? Birthdays?

RUTH   Yeah. Do I get my presents now?

JACK   Sorry, Pinky. No presents till after the guests leave.

RUTH Pleeeeeeeease, Pinky?

JACK Oh all right. One present.

RUTH So what did you get me? Huh? Whadja get me?

JACK Well you know they just issued the trombone sonatas of Arthur Honegger.

RUTH Mmmm-hmmm . . . ?

JACK And I know how much you love Honegger.

RUTH Honegger, off-egger.

JACK Oh, very good! Ten points!

RUTH *Sechel.* (*Pronounced "sayk'l"*)

JACK *Sechel.* What's that, Jewish pastry?

RUTH Jewish brains.

JACK You are such a clever people, thinking up words like *sechel,* and bagel . . .

RUTH But to tell you the truth, I didn't want the Honegger tromboner.

JACK What? You *didn't*??

RUTH & JACK *Uh-oh!*

JACK What *do* you want?

RUTH Just hand over the loot, will ya?

JACK (*Takes a small box from under the bed*) Say "antidisestablishmentarianism."

RUTH Antidisestablishmentarianism.

JACK (*Handing it over*) Happy birthday.

RUTH Hee hee hee. Oh God I do love presents. I do, I do, I do . . . (*She tears off the gift-wrapping.*)   Is it a boat? Is it a train? Is it a plane? (*She sees what's inside the box.*)   Oh, Pinky! A pair of Droopy Eyes! (*It's a pair of trick glasses—the kind in which the eyes hang out of the frames on long springs. She puts them on.*)   How did you know?

JACK I thought you'd want them to go with your blue dress.

RUTH Gosh, thanks, Pinky.

JACK Anything for you, Pinky. (*Kiss*)

RUTH If the real present is like this, I am going to kill you.

JACK Would it be all over?

RUTH It would be *all over*.

JACK Oh, all right. Just to assuage your insatiable rapaciosity.

RUTH Rapaciositudinousness.

JACK Try this. (*He takes another, similar box from under the bed.*)

RUTH Oh but you shouldn't have.

JACK But I did.

RUTH But you shouldn't have.

JACK But I did.

RUTH It looks like the same box.

JACK So open it.

RUTH I thought you'd never ask. Is it a boat? Is it a train? Is it a plane? (*She sees what's inside.*)   Oh God, Jack . . . (*She takes a wristwatch out of the box.*)

JACK A homely little timepiece. Waterproof. Dustproof. Lustproof. You can have sex in that watch—does not affect it.

RUTH Oh *God* . . . !

JACK God? Who? No such entity.

RUTH This is incredible!

JACK So what do you expect from tall, thin, and tasteful people?

RUTH How could you afford this?

JACK Oh, I sold a couple more quarts down at the blood bank.

RUTH (*Holding out her wrist*) Time on my hands. (*Putting it at her side*) Time on my side.

JACK You should put on the Droopy Eyes. It was meant as an ensemble.

RUTH Can I attack you?

JACK Attack me. Make my body your bombing target. (*He opens his arms wide and she jumps into them. They fall onto the bed together.*) Yes! Yes! More sex, you lusty wench!

RUTH Oh God I'm happy!

JACK Hey, I thought you were attacking me. What happened?

RUTH I don't think I've ever been as happy as I am right now.

JACK Actually you've been this happy in the arms of a dozen men. You've just forgotten.

RUTH Stop that now.

JACK Just as you'll forget me some day.

RUTH Cynic.

JACK Pollyanna.

RUTH Fatalist.

JACK Running dog of bourgeois optimism—*Wow! Nice watch!*

RUTH God, it's crazy.

JACK Well sure, everything's crazy.

RUTH I mean it's ironic.

JACK Everything's ironic, if you look at it the right way. What's crazy and ironic today?

RUTH I was just thinking how this guy pursued me for months and I never went to bed with him, and then I saw you *twice* and *I* paid for both of the movies, and bang! Ten days that shook the bed.

JACK Who was this?

RUTH Just a guy.

JACK And he pursued you for months and you never went to bed with him?

RUTH Hey hey hey. It wasn't *entirely* platonic.

JACK Oh. How far did he get?

RUTH Excuse me?

JACK How far did he get? First base? Second base? Shortstop?

RUTH It's none of your busin—Shortstop?

JACK Yeah.

RUTH What's shortstop?

JACK   You know what shortstop is.

RUTH   I didn't go to an all-boy's Catholic school.

JACK   Shortstop is when you—

RUTH   Never mind. I don't want to know.

JACK   So did he get to third base?

RUTH   *We got called on account of rain.* How's that.

JACK   Hee hee hee.

RUTH   Is there anything but sex for you?

JACK   Nope. Freud was right. Everything is sex.

RUTH   Oh yeah? What about love?

JACK   Love? Love?

RUTH   Yeah, remember love?

JACK   That hormonal scam?

RUTH   Rather an important factor in the world, bub.

JACK   No, no, no. *I'll* tell you what's important.

RUTH   Okay. Tell me what's important.

JACK   *Like.* And like-*ness.* People who like the same things
        and are alike. Two people in a bed who really *like* each
        other. Forget about love songs. In my utopia, there'd be *like*
        songs. Volumes of *like* poetry.

RUTH   No love, even in utopia?

JACK   I'd have it confiscated at the border.

RUTH   You don't really mean that.

JACK I absolutely mean that. You think there'd be love in utopia? After all the damage it's done to the world?

RUTH *Especially* in utopia there'd be love.

JACK Why. State your case succinctly and give examples.

RUTH Well . . .

JACK Yes?

RUTH Give me a second here.

JACK I'd love to hear the case for love.

RUTH Well, in utopia you're supposed to be out of danger, right? I mean, you're supposed to be secure in utopia.

JACK Okay. And . . . ?

RUTH And that's what love makes you feel.

JACK Secure?

RUTH Invulnerable. Like nothing could touch you. Like you're protected against death and sickness and unhappiness and the ravages of time and the dog at the door.

JACK I thought love was supposed to make you feel vulnerable.

RUTH No, getting *dumped* makes you feel vulnerable. Not falling in love.

JACK Well I'll go for intense *like*. And intense alikeness. *Gleich mit gleich gesellt sich gern.*

RUTH Translate, *bitte.*

JACK "Like with like goes happily together."

RUTH Into English, I mean.

JACK   "Similar people go together naturally."

RUTH   Sounds like something the Germans would say.

JACK   Oops.

RUTH   A nation of potato people. Nazi potato people. And very, very unfunny.

JACK   My great-grandmother was German.

RUTH   Was she funny?

JACK   Not really.

RUTH   I rest my case.

JACK   No, no. I loved Grandma Shtuckelschwanz.

RUTH   Uh—you *loved* her?

JACK   I intensely liked her. What. What's this look?

RUTH   Jack . . .

JACK   Yes?

RUTH   Will you marry me?

Phone rings.

RUTH (*cont.*)   But speaking of birthdays . . .

JACK   Birthdays, birthdays . . . ?

RUTH   Do I get my presents now?

JACK   Sorry, Pinky. No presents till after the guests leave.

RUTH   Pleeeeeeeeease, Pinky?

JACK   Oh, all right. One present. (*He produces a small box.*)   Say "antidisestablishmentarianism."

RUTH Antidisestablishmentarianism.

JACK Happy birthday.

RUTH Oh God, I do love presents. I do, I do, I do . . . Is it a
boat? Is it a train? Is it a plane? (*Seeing what's inside*) Oh,
God, Nicky . . .

JACK Yes, Nora?

RUTH *The Pearl Fishers.* (*We start to hear the music rising.*)
Two whole discs and a *free booklet?* How could you afford
this?

JACK Oh, I sold a couple more quarts down at the blood
bank. Paradise, yes?

RUTH Paradise absolutely. (*They start to dance.*) Is this a
couple, or what?

JACK No, this is the same person—twice.

RUTH Pinky, what do you say we do this forever. Don't you
think we could? I mean—

JACK Do this forever?

RUTH Yeah. I mean, doesn't this make you think . . . ?

*Music fades out. Jack finds an open bottle of champagne and two
glasses and fills them.*

JACK You mean doesn't it make me think I could reconsider
my usual dark and nasty ideas about the abominable
institution of marriage?

RUTH Something like that.

JACK Doesn't this make me think I could find wed-lock less
than asphyxiating?

RUTH   Something along those lines.

JACK   And that children were not designed by some wicked deity to scream in your ear, pee in your hand, and bankrupt you?

RUTH   Excuse me. You're bankrupt already.

JACK   That's because I was married once.

RUTH   No, that's because you think you can live on two thousand dollars a year.

JACK   So call me an idealist.

RUTH   Freeloader.

JACK   Capitalist.

RUTH   We've started off so beautifully, Jack!

JACK   Six months? What's that?

RUTH   Six months is a lot of time to get to know a person.

JACK   Not even the "t" in "tick" on eternity's clock.

RUTH   I'm not saying we have to run off and hire a JP.

JACK   Jewish JP.

RUTH   You know we're not twenty-five anymore.

JACK   What? We're *not*?

RUTH & JACK   *Uh-oh!*

RUTH   And we won't get to play Romeo and Juliet in bed forever.

JACK   If we got married we wouldn't do *anything* in bed— forever. Anyway, you'd have to get your parents to talk to me first.

RUTH My parents aren't the question.

JACK Just because my name doesn't end in *-berg, -stein,* or *-erkowitz.*

RUTH My parents aren't the question.

JACK I can't believe they agreed to come over tonight.

RUTH My parents aren't the question.

JACK Even though your mother boiled her hand after I shook it? Even though your father hangs garlic around his neck every time he sees me? Even though they threatened to write you out of their *will* if you marry someone who isn't Jewish?

RUTH All right, all right . . .

JACK Christ. *Religion.*

RUTH I know . . .

JACK & RUTH (*Together*) *Superstition and slavery.*

JACK Well that's all religion is. Superstition and slavery.

RUTH Yes I think I've heard this speech before.

JACK And the megabites destroyed the corned-beef-hashemites . . .

RUTH (*Under his next words*) Can we stop this?

JACK . . . and the overbites slew the philobytes because they worshipped a different god.

RUTH Oh, you lapsed Catholic boys. You are quite a crew.

JACK Excuse me, but I am *not* a Catholic.

RUTH Okay, lapsed Catholic.

JACK   Un-de-post-*ex*-lapsed.

RUTH   So, moderately lapsed.

JACK   Haven't your parents noticed that Semitic lips haven't touched yours since that guy at college who had a sex-change operation?

RUTH   They caught on, all right. That's what they're worried about.

JACK   My parents don't mind that you're Jewish.

RUTH   I give your goyish folks a first-class case of the Hebrew-jebrews.

JACK   My folks have never said a single thing about you being Jewish!

RUTH   Maybe not outwardly. But inwardly they mind very *much* that I'm Jewish.

JACK   Oh, *inwardly*.

RUTH   That deafening silence at the table when any reference to my being Jewish came up?

JACK   There are a lot of silences at my parents' table about a lot of things. That's what "goyish" means.

RUTH   That killing politeness?

JACK   Oh, it's their *politeness* that persecuted you. Maybe if your parents wore glasses with little dark wigs and big noses painted on the lenses they could see me as one of their own kind.

RUTH   No stereotypes, please.

JACK   Oh right. This from the girl who planned the How-To-Be-Jewish kit.

RUTH That was in a moment of drunken abandon.

JACK Well, that excuses it.

Swiftly rising heat.

RUTH But did I say that or did you say that?

JACK You said that.

RUTH Well, I can say that. You can't.

JACK Oh yeah? Why?

RUTH Because I'm the one who's saying it.

JACK What makes it acceptable in your mouth and sacrilege in mine? How come you can insult the Germans and the French but your own goddamn tribe is so sacred?

The phone rings loudly once. Abruptly back to calmer rhythm.

RUTH Parents, parents, everything's parents. Who invented parents, anyway?

JACK J. Robert Oppenheimer. You know in *my* utopia, parents wouldn't be *allowed* at birthday parties. It'd be illegal. They'd be ticketed and towed away.

RUTH Mmmm. Great plan.

JACK I mean what century are we in, anyway? What. What's this look?

RUTH Nothing. Just tell me I'm beautiful.

JACK You are *extremely* beautiful. For your age.

RUTH You dog!

JACK Oh, maybe a little crow's-foot here and there . . .

RUTH You hound! You beast! (*Sudden swoon*) Oh Nicky . . .

JACK   Oh Nora . . .

They swoon into bed together and embrace, but—

RUTH   Christ, it's six o'clock! We have to get dressed!

She runs into the bathroom. Jack stares at the place on the bed where she was, as if she's just disappeared.

JACK   Nora . . . ? *Nora* . . . ? OH GOD, NORA!!! WHERE ARE YOU??!

RUTH   Six o'clock, pal. (*Looks into the room*)   I learned that from my *new watch*.

JACK   Plenty of time, plenty of time . . .

RUTH   Rise 'n' shine, lover.

JACK   "'Tis true, 'tis day; what though it be?
       O wilt thou therefore rise from me?
       Why should we rise because 'tis light?
       Did we lie down because 'twas night?"

RUTH   Burma-Shave.

JACK   Philistine.

RUTH   Bookworm.

JACK   Boor.

RUTH   Don't you want to wash up in here? Scrape off some of the funk?

Jack starts to dress.

JACK   No, I want to reek of sex. I want everybody exchanging furtive glances across the room and wondering why the place smells like an aquarium.

RUTH   (*In bathroom*)   Like a what?

JACK   An aquarium.

RUTH (*Puts her head into the room*)   If you tell the aquarium joke tonight, I'll kill you.

JACK   Who, me?

RUTH   Yeah, you.

JACK   Would it be all over?

RUTH   It would *definitely* be all over.

JACK   It seems to take so little these days. Where are the fifty-year attachments of yesteryear? Lost to the weekend liaison.

RUTH   No, lost to the search for the liaison d'être. Raison d'être, liaison d'être . . . ?

JACK   Ouch, ouch.

RUTH   Hee hee hee. You don't know how long I've been saving that up.

JACK   Hey what've you got playing on your inner radio?

RUTH   Let me tune in. (*Puts fingers to her temples, as if listening*)   Bizet. *The Pearl Fishers.*

JACK   Ah! *Les Pêcheurs de perles.* I've had Cyndi Lauper singing "Time after Time" for about three days, and she is driving me crazy, right . . . here. (*Taps the center of his forehead*) "Time after . . .Time after . . .Time after . . ." Give me a coupla bars of Bizet and drive her off the inner radio, will you?

RUTH (*Sings*)   "*Oui, c'est elle!*"

JACK & RUTH (*Sing together*)   "*C'est la déesse plus charmante et plus belle!*"

Ruth stops singing but Jack goes on, standing on the bed to vocalize dramatically as the music rises underneath.

JACK *"Oui, c'est elle!*
         C'est la déesse qui descend parmi nous—"
(*He and the music stop.*)   What's the matter? I'm pearl-fishing by myself here, suddenly.

RUTH I had a thought the other day.

JACK Think it for me.

RUTH Didn't somebody say, "Hell is other people" . . . ?

JACK Sartre the Fartre.

RUTH Hell isn't other people. Hell is *remembering* other people.

JACK I don't quite follow you, Senator.

RUTH I mean getting them stuck in your memory. Having to remember certain conversations over and over again. The scenes that keep coming back. The fights, and the accusations. Running them over and over and over again like a piece of music that you can't get out of your head. That's what I call hell.

JACK That's what I call "Ode on a Grecian Urn." "Forever wilt thou love, and she be fair . . . Forever wilt thou love, and she be fair . . . Forever . . . Forever . . . Forever . . ."

The music fades up.

RUTH Hell isn't other people. Hell is remembering other people. (*The phone rings loudly once and the music stops abruptly.*)   Aren't you going to get dressed?

JACK I *am* getting dressed. Pants. Shirt. Even socks. If I can find them.

RUTH   I mean dressed.

JACK   Your friends wouldn't recognize me if I wore anything fancier than this. They'd think you dumped me for some capitalist and they'd all come up to me and say, "Did you get a load of that loser she was going out with? Thank God she dumped *that* one, boy."

RUTH   Oh, and by the way, Savonarola.

JACK   Uh-oh! I don't like the sound of that at *all*.

RUTH   You be nice to Esther tonight.

JACK   But you know how I love Esther Trendstein.

RUTH   *Tenn*stein.

JACK   Despite her being a complete maroon.

RUTH   One of these days you're going to slip and really call her that.

JACK   Trendstein? Or a maroon?

RUTH   I mean it. None of your usual tonight.

JACK   I will be Mr. Charm.

RUTH   You said that the last time, and you left the room every time she was in it.

JACK   Do you think she noticed?

RUTH   I think she got the idea.

JACK   Maybe it was the trumpet I blew for my exits. What *I* don't understand is how you and that gold-plated JAP ever got to be friends in the first place. (*Ruth says nothing.*) Winner of the Golden Palm de Boredom. (*She still says nothing.*)   Do I hear a silence?

RUTH   You know I hate that word.

JACK   Boredom?

RUTH   *JAP.*

JACK   Do you deny that Esther is a Jewish American Princess?

RUTH   It doesn't matter what she is. I still hate it.

JACK   It's the only term that applies. Anyway, Esther hates me too, so it's mutual.

RUTH   She doesn't hate you.

JACK   She thinks I'm a loser, which is the same thing.

RUTH   But you *are* a loser, darling!

JACK   Oh well, that's all right, then.

RUTH   Teaching math to fourteen-year-olds for odd change and a school lunch?

JACK   But the lunches are so good.

RUTH   You're not exactly Mr. Solvent.

JACK   Who ever said I wanted to be? Who ever said I *should* be?

RUTH   Nothing wrong with a few comforts.

JACK   I have all the comforts I need, thank you.

RUTH   Like that rathole of an apartment?

JACK   Rathole? Rathole?

RUTH   Okay. Parakeet cage.

JACK   Maybe it's a parakeet cage but it's certainly not a rathole. Besides, there's plenty of room over here.

RUTH   Is that what you call comfort?

JACK   In my life there is simplicity, there is integrity, there is unattachment to the things of this world. I ask myself: What do I need? To Esther Trendstein, the human steam shovel, who asks what can she *get,* these things make me Quasimodo the bell ringer. Unlike the toilet paper tycoon she married.

RUTH   *Waxed* paper.

JACK   The Jewish Prince Charming. The sheikh of West Ninety-ninth Street. (*Middle Eastern accent*)   "Let me show you my tent. My sheep. My flocks of goats. My beautiful wife. I own her. I have branded my name into her forehead. Someday she will bear me a son. Then I will roast her and eat her."

RUTH   That's not a sheikh. You sound like Dracula.

JACK   "Have I told you that my toilet paper company earned over four-point-five zillion dollars last year? Today I bought the entire state of Montana for my summer home."

RUTH   What do you want, he's an Israeli.

JACK   Ah-*ha*! Anti-Semitism!

RUTH   I can say that. You can't.

JACK   You know what Esther gave him for Hanukkah?

RUTH   I'm afraid to ask.

JACK   His dick, in a small box.

RUTH   Jack . . .

JACK   My lips are sealed. In wax.

RUTH   You are *impossible.*

JACK   I'm not even probable, but I'm here. I think. Am I? Remind me. Flash me one of those gorgeous gams, why don'tcha. (*She sticks one leg out.*)   Oh God, I'm young again. I swear if I had ten lives I'd spend one of them just watching you put on your stockings.

RUTH   Is there anything but sex for you?

JACK   Nope. Freud was right. Everything is sex. Except sex, which is money. Which is actually feces. But everything else is sex. The world is ruled by hormones. Estrogen. Endrogen. Nitrogen. Bombay gin.

RUTH   You know there's nothing wrong with a few comforts and a little security.

JACK   Hey, it's not like I haven't had money-making nonloser ideas in my life.

RUTH   Oh, like the grunge rock toothpaste?

JACK   "Deca-Dent"?

RUTH   The bumper stickers? "Have a Nice Bidet"—? Or "Cockers, the prophylactic for dogs"?

JACK   Market those right and I could make a million, and Esther would mess her Hammacher Schlemmer diapers.

RUTH   What is this *mishigaas* men always have about their girlfriends' friends?

JACK   *Mishigaas? Moi?*

RUTH   It's so weird. At least you like Bob and Sandy.

JACK   I love Bob and Sandy. But that's because they're tall, thin, and funny, like us.

RUTH   You like Morrie and Jean.

JACK   I adore Morrie and Jean.

RUTH And Harry and Robin.

JACK I venerate Harry and Robin.

RUTH I wish we could've had some of *your* friends at the party.

JACK I don't have any friends. Not to call up, anyway.

RUTH It's true, isn't it . . .

JACK Only to hang up on.

RUTH Why is that? Why don't you have any friends?

JACK You're my friend. You and the fourteen-year-olds. Good *God*!

RUTH What.

JACK What are those things you're putting on your feet?

RUTH They are called shoes in my language.

JACK I recognized the general species, but—*blue shoes*?

RUTH What's wrong with them?

JACK BLUE SHOES?

RUTH Yeah. Blue shoes.

JACK Do you *need* a pair of blue shoes?

RUTH Hey, it's my birthday, Mr. Walden Pond.

JACK Tell that to the starving children of India.

RUTH Socialist.

JACK Socialite.

The phone rings.

JACK & RUTH (*Together*) *Telephone, sweetie!*

JACK It's probably the Save the Shoes Committee. (*The phone rings again.*)

RUTH No, somebody's probably late.

JACK (*Picks up the receiver*) Gotham porno line, Pinky speaking.—Hello? (*Listens*) I know you're there, sir. I can hear you breathing.

RUTH Jack, give me that. (*Into phone*) Hi, Dad. Sorry about that . . .

JACK Hee hee hee . . .

RUTH (*Shushing Jack; into phone*) What's up? Chronically late again, or—? Oh . . . Uh-huh. Uh-huh . . . No, it's *not* all right, actually . . . Well, I hope you're going to change your—I said I hope you're going to change your mind.— Okay. Okay. No, don't call me later in the week. I said *don't* call me. 'Bye!

She bangs down the receiver.

JACK What's the matter?

RUTH They're not coming.

JACK Oh. Did he bother to make any flimsy excuses?

RUTH No.

JACK Did he say *anything*?

RUTH He said they'd take me out to dinner later in the week.

JACK Well that was nice of him.

RUTH I'm sorry.

JACK   Don't be sorry.

RUTH   I'm sorry anyway, I feel sorry. God, they can be such *assholes*.

JACK   Well sure. They're parents. And *you* don't have anything to be sorry about.

RUTH   They're just my parents. That's all.

JACK   You know, I could leave if you want.

RUTH   What . . . ?

JACK   So that they could come to your party. I'd be happy to take a walk. Hit a movie.

RUTH   Don't be crazy. (*Pause*)   I don't know what I'm going to tell people when my parents don't show up.

JACK   Tell them the truth. Say your father's rounding up a posse for me down at B'nai B'rith. Does anyone expect a woman of your, ah, age to have her parents at her birthday party anyway? It's not like we're bobbing for apples here.

RUTH   I could just kill him.

JACK   Oh what the hell. Say "antidisestablishmentarianism." (*She says nothing.*)   Say "pork bellies." (*She says nothing.*)   Say "vagina."

RUTH   Vagina.

JACK   Say it happier.

RUTH   Vagina.

JACK   Say "magic fingers."

RUTH   Magic fingers.

JACK   Say—(*She kisses him.*)   Don't say a word. You are cured. Arise, take up thy pallet and go.

RUTH   Oh shut up.

JACK   And behold, he did shut up.

RUTH   You know what I should have said to him?—Never mind. It's not important.

JACK   The French have a term for that.

RUTH   For what.

JACK   Stairway thoughts.

RUTH   Stairway thoughts? What's the English for that?

JACK   It's what you think of when you're out on the stairs going down and you realize what you should've said to the bastard back there. Stairway thoughts.

RUTH   Trust the French.

JACK   *Esprit d'escalier.*

RUTH   Don't be pedantic.

JACK   Hey, don't blame me, blame the French. Is everything ready in the kitchen?

RUTH   We just have to put it all out.

JACK   You okay?

RUTH   No. Just a small case of the weepies.

JACK   Come on. Don't let it get you down.

RUTH   Of course it's going to get me down.

JACK   They're just parents.

RUTH   Yes, and they just insulted the hell out of you.

JACK   I'm not hurt.

RUTH   Oh, sure. Sure.

JACK   Okay, I'm hurt and I hate the bastards and I think we'll have more fun without 'em. This way I won't have to fight your father for the chip dip. Chip . . . *dip*?

RUTH   I didn't even really want them here, I just invited them to be nice. To be a *good daughter.* Why do I always do that? Don't I ever learn?

JACK   They're just parents. The hell with 'em.

RUTH   Parents, parents . . . Who invented parents, anyway.

JACK   Psychiatrists. But who invented children? Ha! Can you answer me *that* question, Professor? Those beings designed by some wicked deity to scream in your ear, pee in your hand, and bankrupt you? (*Very distantly, we hear the echo of a phone ring.*)   What. What's this gimlet-eyed look?

RUTH   I want them sometime, you know. Kids, I mean.

JACK   I know.

RUTH   The two of us could make wonderful kids, Pinky.

JACK   We *are* wonderful kids.

RUTH   We could breed a whole crop of tall, thin, and funny children. The vanguard in that utopian future when everybody will be tall, thin, and funny. And we'd be the ones who started it.

JACK   What do you do if they end up short, fat, and dull?

RUTH   You stretch 'em, put 'em on a diet, and teach 'em some jokes.

JACK Well if they were *my* kids, your mother would have them kidnapped and sent to a kibbutz for deprogramming. And bye-bye utopia.

RUTH You know that's why Bob and Sandy went to Aruba.

JACK To join a kibbutz?

RUTH To make a baby.

JACK Oh.

RUTH We're not twenty-five anymore, Jack.

JACK Well listen, you have to be your thin, witty, and charming self in about fifteen minutes, so you'd better get it together. People will think we've been having a serious conversation.

RUTH We do have a good time together, don't we.

JACK Sure. We're friends. Remember? So hey. Since we *are* such good friends . . . you wanna fuck, pal?

RUTH Ohhhhhhhhh no . . .

JACK Oh yes, he said, yes yes yes!

RUTH None of that! Get away from me, you fiend!

JACK Come on, just a quickie.

RUTH Why does this always happen right before a party?

JACK One final embracement.

RUTH You always say that and we're always late.

JACK We've never regretted it yet.

RUTH You have to do something about this chronic horniness.

JACK   It's my tragic flaw. Horniness is next to tardiness. (*Suddenly pointing in the air as a diversionary tactic*)   Look! (*She looks, he dives across the bed, she eludes him.*)

RUTH   Everybody's coming *here* this time.

JACK   So we'll let 'em in and they can watch.

RUTH   Jack . . .

JACK   It'll be the real thing, right in front of their eyes. The beatific vision. The second coming. Or third or fourth. So come on, what do you say? Huh? Hm? Huh? Bed? Sex? Bed?

RUTH   Will you ever grow up?

JACK   Nope. Come on. You'll love it. So will I. What do you say?

RUTH   Do you promise we'll be quick?

JACK   Scout's honor. Two hours or under.

RUTH   One foot on the floor at all times?

JACK   And both hands on the ceiling. Deal?

RUTH   You're on.

They start to undress. The doorbell rings. They stop.

JACK   We could still do it really quick.

RUTH   Sorry, pal. Fate has spoken. (*She pulls her clothing back together.*)

JACK   Oh my balls are going to be sapphire blue all night.

RUTH   Good. They'll match my shoes. (*Doorbell*)   *Just a minute!*

JACK   Last chance.

RUTH   Down, Casanova. And remember what I said.

JACK   Right.—What did you say?

RUTH   Are you ready to face the world? Testicles tucked in?

JACK (*Facing a firing squad*)   You may fire when ready, captain.

RUTH   Paradise?

JACK   Absolutely.

Ruth opens the door and suddenly the lights change and there's loud party music. Ruth and Jack dance to it. Then Ruth shuts the door and the lights change back and the music stops.

JACK   Wooooeeee!

RUTH (*Jive talk*)   *Everybody* lookin' good!

JACK   That was one hell of a party, Pinkerstein.

RUTH   Oh you think so?

JACK   I do, I do, I do. I definitely do. The bash of the year. (*They collapse onto the bed.*)   Are we something?

RUTH   We are something all right. What are we again?

JACK   Expert party-givers.

RUTH   Oh, right. Right. I forgot . . .

JACK   But where did everybody go? The happy guests sure bailed out of here fast.

RUTH   I know. I thought my apartment had hit an iceberg.

JACK   We have to do this every year.

RUTH   Well. Guess we might as well start excavating. (*She starts up.*)

JACK   Aw, leave it for tomorrow. Come on and give your old pal a nuzzle. Come on. (*He puts his arms around her.*)

RUTH   Nuzzle nuzzle.

JACK   And may I say, you looked fabulous tonight.

RUTH   For my age. I know.

JACK   No, no. I spent the whole evening with a hardy niblick in my trousers, just looking at you. Maybe it was the expensive blue shoes.

RUTH   I'll never hear the end of them, will I.

JACK   I wanted to make passionate love with you right on the floor, but Esther had covered it with tortilla chips. No doubt part of a plot to keep us apart.

RUTH   By the way, Mr. Bernstein.

JACK   Yes, Mr. Kane?

RUTH   You were terrific. Thank you.

JACK   Oh, thanks. You were terrific too. What were we terrific about?

RUTH   I mean with Esther.

JACK   (*As if trying to remember*)   Esther, Esther . . .

RUTH   I couldn't believe how nice you were being. I mean, actually talking to her—?

JACK   It wasn't that hard. I was wearing earplugs.

RUTH   I mean it, Jack.

JACK   Well, *she started it*. She sure was in a bouncy mood tonight.

RUTH   Mmmmmm.

JACK Disgustingly bouncy. And the sheikh seemed absolutely ecstatic. As usual, I got treated to the condensed version of the Joys of Yiddish. (*With accent*) "And this *schmeggege* was *ganz* meshuga, so I took my mezuzah and I hit him on the *Kopf*."

RUTH I'm going to get out of these clothes.

JACK Now you're talking. Just let me get my binoculars in focus, while the hostess disrobes. (*He puts his hands to his eyes like binoculars. She starts to undress.*) Sandy looked good tonight.

RUTH Sandy looked great.

JACK Was the trip to Aruba successful? Is she with child?

RUTH They don't know yet. They're buying that apartment, though.

JACK How boozhy. (*Ruth stops undressing and stands very still.*) What.

RUTH Nothing.

JACK What.

RUTH Just got tired all of a sudden.

JACK Lucy looked good.

RUTH Lucy? Lucy looked *awful*.

JACK You're right. She did look pretty awful.

RUTH All pasty-faced and wrinkled. That's what comes of living alone for ten years.

JACK And whatever happened to what's-their-name, the fortune cookies?

RUTH The fortune cookies had a fight and begged off.

JACK Of course. They're married—they had a fight. A syllogism.

RUTH Do you realize we've never had a fight? We never shout, we never brawl . . . What the hell is wrong with us?

JACK We're not made to fight. We're made to love. We . . . are made . . . to *love*.

RUTH Excuse me, Cupid. You don't believe in love. Remember?

JACK What? I *don't*?

RUTH & JACK *Uh-oh!*

JACK You are so *schlegel*. Always catching me out like that.

RUTH Have you ever thought you should be going out with Lucy?

JACK Me? What? Go out with Lucy?

RUTH Yeah. Or somebody like Lucy?

JACK Gad*zooks*!

RUTH I mean, she's goyish, and you're goyish . . .

JACK Oh. So Lucy and I should buy a white clapboard house in Connecticut and *goy* together. Is that the idea?

RUTH Just a thought.

JACK I'm going out with *you*. Remember?

RUTH Oh yeah. *Duhh.*

JACK *Duhh.*

Now he starts to undress and change back into his robe, scattering his clothes around the room as they were at the beginning of the play. She hangs her blue dress in the bathroom doorway, as it was at the start of the play, and gets into her robe.

JACK Hey, what was all that between you and Esther?

RUTH What was what?

JACK What was all that stuff about temple?

RUTH She wants me to come to her temple for Rosh Hashanah.

JACK Why?

RUTH What do you mean, why.

JACK You're not going to go, are you?

RUTH Uh-huh.

JACK To Rosh Hashanah services?

RUTH Of course I'm going.

JACK What for? When was the last time you went to Rosh Hashanah services?

RUTH I go to Rosh Hashanah services every year.

JACK Oh. I see.

RUTH It's not a felony, Inspector. It's Rosh Hashanah services.

JACK But you don't believe all that stuff.

RUTH It doesn't have anything to do with believing.

JACK So what does it have to do with?

RUTH It doesn't have anything to do with believing.

JACK   So what does it have to do with?

RUTH   It doesn't have anything to do with believing.

JACK   Superstition and slavery.

RUTH   Yes I think I've heard this speech someplace before.

JACK   This month, Rosh Hashanah services; next month, the ritual baths to purify your uncleanness. Then what? You shave your head and start saying all those prayers thanking God you're not a woman?

RUTH   You don't know what you're talking about, buddy.

JACK   Okay. I don't know what I'm talking about.

RUTH   You're more than welcome to come along to Rosh Hashanah services.

JACK   Oh sure. I can see that.

RUTH   I *am* Jewish, you know.

JACK   Jewish? No. You're tallish, thinnish, and funnyish. Remember? Ish?

RUTH   Did anybody call tonight?

JACK   No. Not that I know of. Not that I heard. Why.

RUTH   Nothing.

JACK   Do you think you won the lottery?

RUTH   Do you know that he didn't even wish me a happy birthday?

JACK   Who?

RUTH   When he called?—My father.

JACK   Oh. Well, maybe we didn't hear the phone with all the racket.

RUTH   I know it's stupid.

JACK   It's not stupid.

RUTH   Stupid stuff . . . And you know what I should've said to him? Forget it. It's not important.

JACK   The French have a term for that, you know. Stairway thoughts.

RUTH   Trust the French.

JACK   Hey. It's not *their* fault they're French.

RUTH   *Collaborators* . . . He couldn't even wish me a happy birthday.

Jack comes up behind her and kisses the back of her neck.

JACK   Happy birthday, babe. I'll make up the difference. (*Kisses her neck again. She turns and looks at him hard.*)   What. What's this gimlet-eyed look.

RUTH   Nothing.

JACK   Forgot what I looked like again, huh.

RUTH   Jack, make it stop.

JACK   What . . . ?

RUTH   Make it stop. *Make it stop. Make it stop.*

The phone rings, once. The music fades up, briefly.

JACK   Forgot what I looked like again, huh.

RUTH   Never. Never, ever.

Music fades out.

JACK (*Continues undressing*) Hey, who's this guy Josh who was here tonight?

RUTH Josh?

JACK Yeah. *Josh.*

RUTH Oh, he's an old friend . . .

JACK You seemed very surprised to see him, for an old friend.

RUTH I didn't expect him to be here. He's a doctor.

JACK "I didn't expect him to be here—he's a doctor." Somehow the logic of that escapes me. (*She says nothing.*) Is this that platonic guy you were going out with . . . ?

RUTH No, no, it's not him.

JACK Well whoever Josh is, he certainly seemed interested in my living arrangements. Kept asking me if I *lived* here. I wondered if he was looking for a share. Or a date. (*She says nothing.*) So?

RUTH So what.

JACK So who is this mystery guest?

RUTH Esther and I met him at her cousin's anniversary thing.

JACK What, a couple of months ago? Not exactly what I'd call an old friend.

RUTH I think she knew him from before, somehow.

JACK Uh-huh. And—let me guess. You met him at Esther's cousin's anniversary thing, and he asked you out. (*Ruth says nothing.*) Did he ask you out?

RUTH He did, actually.

JACK So what did you do?

RUTH   I said I was going out with somebody else.

JACK   And?

RUTH   And what?

JACK   You tell him you're going out with somebody else, so he shows up at your birthday party?

RUTH   He's just been calling me up every once in a while.

JACK   Oh.

RUTH   Look. I didn't expect him to be here tonight. Esther brought him.

JACK   What for?

RUTH   I don't know.

JACK   Did you ever go out with him?

RUTH   No!

JACK   Just asking. Just asking.

RUTH   There's no need to be jealous or anything.

JACK   I'm not jealous.

RUTH   He'd call me up every once in a while to talk. That's all.

JACK   Okay.

RUTH   At the office.

JACK   Okay.

RUTH   I didn't call *him*.

JACK   Okay. (*He undresses in silence a moment.*)

RUTH   Are you upset?

JACK   No.

RUTH   So what are you?

JACK   Well, I'm not surprised anyway. Everybody I've ever gone out with has done this.

RUTH   Done what.

JACK   Kept somebody in reserve. Kept somebody around for just-in-case-things-don't-work-out.

RUTH   I wasn't keeping him in reserve, Jack!

JACK   Oh come on, Ruth.

RUTH   I wasn't!

JACK   Come on. Everybody does it. Keeps somebody around for just-in-case-you-happen-to-break-up.

RUTH   He's nothing. He's nobody.

JACK   It's fine. Really. I'm sorry I asked. I'm sorry I butted in.

RUTH   You didn't butt in on anything.

JACK   This was just a different way of finding out. Usually there's an inopportune phone call, when you pick up instead of her, and you find out that she and some guy have been "just talking on the phone," quote unquote, every week. It's modern life. It's nothing. Big deal.

RUTH   Have *you* been keeping somebody in reserve?

JACK   For once in my life, I haven't. I just wish I hadn't been so fucking nice to Esther tonight. I should've known that any slight advance in civility is just compensation for some sleazeball activity under the table.

RUTH   Oh Christ . . .

JACK No wonder she was in such a bouncy mood tonight. She was matchmaking! Too bad your parents weren't here. Your old man would've paid Doctor Josh cold hard cash to take you off my hands. He's perfect!

RUTH The reason that Esther was in such a "bouncy mood" tonight is that she's pregnant.

JACK Oh.

RUTH *That's* why. They just don't want to announce it yet.

JACK Well great. I'm sure the sheikh must be delighted. He'll probably—

RUTH Don't make any cracks, Jack. Please.

JACK What did you say to her?

RUTH I said I was happy for her.

JACK It seems motherhood is very in.

RUTH Motherhood is in. Marriage is in.

JACK What *century* are we in?

RUTH This one, remember?

JACK But you know Esther isn't going to have just *one* kid. Uh-uh. Any shmo can have one kid—so Esther's going to have five, all at once. And you know what she's going to give birth to, don't you? If she has quintuplets? (*Ruth says nothing.*) You know what Esther's going to give birth to?

RUTH (*Reluctantly*) What.

JACK *Poly*esters. Ha, ha, ha, ha, ha. Is this a clever child?

RUTH I want them sometime too, Jack. I want kids sometime.

JACK I know that.

RUTH The two of us could make wonderful kids, Pinky.

JACK We *are* wonderful kids.

RUTH A whole crop of tall, thin, and funny children.

JACK What'll you do if they end up short, fat, and dull?

RUTH We're not twenty-five anymore.

JACK So I hear. But hey! Did I tell you my new moneymaker? This is going to make me richer than the sheikh. Listen to this: *braille pajamas.* Huh? What do you think? This is for all those nights when you wake up in terror and you don't know where you are. You sit up in the dark and you clutch your heart and you say, "Oh my God, where am I?!" Well, with my pajamas, the answer is pasted over the pocket in braille, so you'd go, "Oh my God, where am I?" (*Stops. Clutches his heart. Suddenly calm*) Oh. I'm with Ruth. In Duluth. Or Oberammergau. Or wherever you happen to be. You're not impressed, I can tell. But think of the million-and-one other items, for people who don't wear pajamas. Braille nighties. Braille boxers. Of course everybody'd have to learn braille. But think how that would promote understanding between the sight-impaired and the sought. So what do you think?

RUTH Jack, will you marry me?

Silence.

JACK I b-b-beg your pardon?

RUTH Will you marry me, Jack?

JACK Come on, Ruth, don't kid around. It's not funny.

RUTH Who's kidding around? Jack, will you marry me?—
Pop quiz.

JACK You mean *marry* you? As in . . . ?

RUTH As in "marry me." As in "marriage." That ancient ruse
to start a home—? Still popular in certain parts of the world,
you know.

JACK You don't want to get married, Ruth.

RUTH I do. To you. Do you?

JACK This is absurd . . . !

RUTH Let me try this again. Jack, will you marry me?

JACK Well hey. This is kinda sudden, Doc.

RUTH It's not like we haven't had time to think about this
over six long and blissful months.

JACK Yeah but I wasn't thinking about it.

RUTH That's okay. *I* was thinking about it.

JACK Six months isn't all that much time, Ruth.

RUTH At our age it's an eternity.

JACK "At our age"? What does that mean?

RUTH It means I'm retiring and going into a nursing home
next week, and I'd love to get married before then.

JACK Six months isn't even long enough for me to find out
you go to Rosh Hashanah services every year! Just think
what we could find out in the *next* six months.

RUTH What will we know in six months that we don't know
now? We know we're crazy about each other. So. Will you
marry me, Jack?

JACK Do I get some time to think about this?

RUTH Sure! Take a minute or two. Take three, they're small.

JACK So I'm supposed to answer this more or less now? Tonight?

RUTH Early tomorrow is fine. Which it already is, according to my lovely new watch.

JACK Okay. Well. First things first. What about your parents, what are they going to say if you—

RUTH (*Over his last words, slightly*) Forget about my parents.

JACK But you don't think your parents are going to let you—

RUTH (*Overlapping slightly*) *Forget* about my parents. I'll take them out to dinner and ply them with sour cream, they'll say yes to anything. So. Will *you* . . . marry *me*? Remember *me*?

JACK Oh Ruth . . .

RUTH You remembered!

JACK You know what this is.

RUTH Um. No. What is this?

JACK You have all your friends over, most of your friends are married, you find out Esther's going to have a baby—power of suggestion! This isn't even you talking.

RUTH I *thought* it was me. Quick check. Yep, it's me all right.

JACK No, no, no. This is Esther, ventriloquizing through you.

RUTH I want a husband, Jack.

JACK Why?

RUTH   I don't know. I like words that start with *h*. Home. Challah. Husband.

JACK   Horrible. *Hello*. Don't you realize we have something extraordinary here?

RUTH   I don't want the extraordinary, terrific as it is. I want the ordinary and secure. I want a husband.

JACK   How terribly traditional.

RUTH   Yes it is traditional. *I'm* traditional. You should know that about me by now.

JACK   Traditional? You?

RUTH   I'm very traditional. I crochet when you're not looking. I preserve pickles in funny-looking jars.

JACK   But you're in the avant-garde of humanity! You're part of the perfect breed of the future!

RUTH   Somehow I don't think I am.

JACK   Tall and thin and funny—?

RUTH   Jack, you ought to be *glad* I'm doing the asking here. I help you out. I give you a place to hang around in that isn't a rathole. Excuse me, a parakeet cage. I get you out into the world. I provide you with a circle of friends. Say but the word and all this is yours. It's a real life, Jack. It's adult life.

JACK   Would marriage help me keep my hair?

RUTH   *Yes*. Or your money back, guaranteed. And it'll give you somebody to curmudge with when you're eighty. Okay, yes, maybe sex will be nasty, poor, brutish, and short.

JACK   When there *is* any.

RUTH   When there is any. But sex is not all there is to life.

JACK   Well . . . It's partly all there is.

RUTH   Isn't somebody beside you in bed better than nobody at all? You can't go from girlfriend to girlfriend forever, you know. After a while you're not going to be boyfriend material. You're going to be a dog's dinner, my son.

JACK   Thank you for that, sweetie.

RUTH   But you could have kids to live with you and not mind that you're a dog's dinner.

JACK   Not if *I* was my kid. If *I* was my kid I wouldn't live with me.

RUTH   Marriage would also lift you up.

JACK   Out of what?

RUTH   To the level you belong on. How can you be a high school math teacher, with everything you know? You could be something wonderful.

JACK   I thought I *was* something wonderful. A math teacher. And secretly a member of the cognoscenti.

RUTH   Right now you're just a cog of the cognoscenti.

JACK   Well, maybe. But *I* put the ram in the ram-a-dam-a-ding-dong.

RUTH   I don't want to get old, Jack.

JACK   Yeah, well. There's nothing you can do about that . . .

RUTH   I don't want to get old all by myself. And I don't want to end up like Lucy, all by herself and losing her looks to loneliness.

JACK   But you can get married and still end up old and alone.

RUTH   Yes, you can walk into the street and get hit by a truck, too. You have to plan *something*, for Christ's sake, otherwise you're just . . . You have to plan *some* things.

JACK   You know, you're right. What's for breakfast?

RUTH   Please be serious for just one minute?

JACK   Look, can I tell you one story about my marriage? The two of us once went on vacation and we—

RUTH   But that was years ago, Jack!

JACK   No, no, no, listen to this.

RUTH   All that stuff is ancient history now! You're a different person!

JACK   You don't know what you're chasing after!

RUTH   I'm chasing after *you*! Against all reason.

JACK   A favorite phrase of horrid ex-wife, "Against all reason."

RUTH   Well I'm sorry but I can't avoid saying and doing things the horrid ex did. You made a mistake getting married at age seven and now it's time to move on. Being married to the horrid ex wasn't *all* marriages.

JACK   It was a very good example.

RUTH   People don't *have* to be unhappily married.

JACK   What? They *don't?*

RUTH   (*Doesn't pick up the routine*)   No. They don't.

JACK   Ruth, do you know any couple as good as we are? No. Listen. Do you know any two who get along as well as we do, minute by minute and inch by inch? Who can hum the Mendelssohn Octet *and* know the Marx Brothers by heart?

RUTH Exactly! If you and I can't make a marriage work, who can? Two people who are the same person? Perfect companions?

JACK But we'd be different, if we got married.

RUTH Why? Why? Why? Why am I different now from what I'd be if I married you?

JACK Because you'd change.

RUTH Ogh!

JACK *I'd* change. We'd both change. We'd turn from Nick and Nora into Dick and Pat Nixon.

RUTH This Pavlov reaction about marriage.

JACK Yes it's a Pavlov reaction, and I have it for a very good reason. Because I've been there. If companionship is what you want, if that's what's important, you can get that without being married. And here I am. Yes. Your perfect companion.

RUTH Kids are important, too.

JACK A friend that you can joke around with.

RUTH Kids are very important.

JACK Sure, except when they pee in your hand.

RUTH *Even* when they pee in your hand. *Especially* when they pee in your hand.

JACK But we'd be lousy parents. We'd be horrible at the job!

RUTH So we'd learn the job. If Imelda Marcos did, we can too.

JACK I'd be a terrible father. You'd be a terrible mother!— What.

RUTH Do you realize what a lousy thing that is to say to somebody?

JACK I'm sorry I said that.

RUTH I can't believe you said that to me.

JACK I'm sorry I said it.

RUTH Well, I guess I have my answer.

JACK No, listen, Ruth . . .

RUTH I have my answer. So what do we do?

The phone rings, once.

JACK Will you marry me, Ruth? Will you marry me?

RUTH Come on. Don't kid around, this isn't funny.

JACK Who's kidding around? We have to get married to stay together? Let's marry, have a Baby Ruth, and move on.

RUTH You don't really mean that.

JACK You want a husband? Here he is! I'll even toss in home and challah. Let's throw on some clothes and go buy a license. Think there's an all–night marriage bureau open somewhere?

RUTH But you don't believe in marriage, remember?

JACK Of course I don't! I refuse to believe in marriage! It's against my principles. But I'll marry you to keep us together. Where's my coat? Come on, babe! Let's go take some vows!

RUTH How can you get married if you don't believe in marriage?

JACK Fish don't believe in water, but they swim in it.

RUTH After all I've heard from you about marriage for six months?

JACK Yes, he said, yes I will he said, yes yes yes.

RUTH Why yes now, after no for so long?

JACK Because you are the exception to every horrible thing that anybody can think about this world—and that I, even *I,* have ever thought about this world. Grass grows in your path where wasteland was before. Double rainbows leap into the sky ahead of you. And we could have one hell of a wedding. I'll wear a sweatshirt that says "Superstition and Slavery" in enormous red letters. And you will go up the aisle in the bluest pair of shoes you ever saw. (*The phone rings loudly, once.*) Marry me, Ruth.

RUTH I'm afraid this is all just a little too easy.

JACK Easy . . . ?

RUTH Well you don't just run off and find a JP. Before we got married, we'd have to agree about certain things.

JACK We always agree about things! I mean, except *some* things, but . . . Name something we have to agree about and I'll agree to it. I'm agreeable.

RUTH We have to think this through.

JACK Well hey, this is romantic. I thought when somebody proposed, people started screaming and crying and falling into each other's arms.

RUTH Okay. Well. I'm not going to marry you if we don't have kids.

JACK I know that. Of course I know that.

RUTH But I don't mean in ten years, Jack. I mean soon.

JACK   What does "soon" mean?

RUTH   It means very soon.

JACK   Are you pregnant?

RUTH   No, I'm not pregnant.

JACK   Look, I wasn't trying to insult you or something—

RUTH   Forget it. Forget it.

JACK   I was just asking.

RUTH   I'm just saying "soon."

JACK   Okay. Soon. I agree. Very soon. We'll call OBGYN in the morning and make an appointment.

RUTH   If we got married we'd also have to find a place big enough for a family to live in. Ultimately we'd have to think about whether we wanted to live in the city at all. And schools. What kind of school, public school, private school . . .

JACK   Hey, hey, hey! The kid's not even born yet!

RUTH   You can't hum the Mendelssohn Octet on two thousand dollars a year anymore, either. It's gone up.

JACK   Well—my two thousand plus your two hundred thousand . . .

RUTH   Married or unmarried, we couldn't hum anything. Not on two thousand dollars a year.

JACK   You know I *do* make more than two thousand doll—

RUTH   Whatever you make. And you may think I make a lot of money at my job but I make nothing.

JACK   You must make something—

RUTH   I make *nothing*. *Nothing*.

JACK   Okay, you make nothing. I make nothing. We both make nothing.

RUTH   Sometime, you know—sooner or later—you'd have to find a different job.

JACK   Different job. Different job . . .

RUTH   Something to raise a family on.

JACK   But I *like* my job. You know that.

RUTH   Yes, I know you like your job, but a family can't live on it. If you want to teach, maybe you can find a better school, or teach at a college. You *should* be teaching in a college.

JACK   Hey, who is this person I'm talking to here? Could I talk to Ruth again, please? The real Ruth?

The phone rings loudly, once.

RUTH   Tell me you'll be miserable without me. Tell me you'll be as miserable without me as I'll be without you. Tell me you'll lie awake at night thinking about me. Tell me when the phone rings you'll still think it might be me.

The phone rings, once.

JACK   This isn't even you talking.

RUTH   Yes, this is me talking.

JACK   Could I talk to Ruth again, please? The real Ruth?

RUTH   You're not going to live off me, Jack.

JACK   *Live* off you . . . ?

RUTH   Okay, okay. I'm sorry I said that.

JACK LIVE OFF YOU?

RUTH Well, you might as well be living *here*. The way you've settled into this apartment.

JACK I thought you *liked* having me over here.

RUTH Since your own apartment is too small to live in.

JACK I have lived in that apartment for many years, thank you. And I haven't been over here for the real estate. I've been here to see you. Remember?

RUTH It's very easy to be a socialist when your girlfriend's got a nice apartment. Do you realize I've even been providing the *friends* in this relationship?

JACK Okay, so I don't have a raft of friends, like you. *You're* my friend.

RUTH We can't invite any of your friends to my party, so you just . . . use mine.

JACK *Use* yours?

RUTH Yes, or however you want to . . .

JACK (*Cutting in on her*) What, have I been getting dirty fingerprints all over your friends or something? Have I been leaving the cap off your tube of acquaintances? Okay, you have a large circle of friends and I don't. What were we supposed to do when we started going out? Exchange friends, like hostages?

RUTH It just says something about you, that you have no friends.

JACK But there's no news here. I don't have a model apartment, I don't have a social calendar. If you wanted somebody normal, toss a brick out the window and you'll

hit one. You know how I live and what I think. So why
did you ask me to marry you?

RUTH   Because I hoped against hope you'd jump in the air
and say yes, and actually make me believe you. Which you
didn't. And I had my answer. I had my answer all right.
Classic Jack.

JACK   Well what the fuck have you been doing with me for
six months?

RUTH   Maybe I hoped you were kidding all that time. That
you'd do away with marriage, and kids, and cars, and
political parties—

JACK   You joined in that game, too—

RUTH   Have you ever stopped and just *listened* to yourself?
You don't believe in this, you don't believe in that, no
private property, no marriage, no religion, no love. Not
even love?! Not even the lowest common denominator?

JACK   Do you want me to say I believe in love? Okay. I
believe in love. Do you want me to say that I love you? I
love you, Ruth. I love you.

The phone rings, once.

RUTH   You don't believe in this, you don't believe in that.
How can you get up from day to day believing in
nothing?

JACK   I don't believe in nothing.

RUTH   How can you live in the world?

JACK   I can live in the world because of people like you.

RUTH   That's very beautiful.

JACK *I can live in the world because of people like you.* What do you want me to say?

RUTH Look, I wasn't . . . I mean that. It's very beautiful. Thank you.

JACK If you want a contract, I can write that in.

RUTH No, a . . . letter of agreement is fine.

JACK Reason for living: Ruth. How can I brush my teeth in the morning? Ruth. How can I stand the idea of eggplant? Ruth. You agree with me on eggplant.

RUTH I agree with you on everything.

JACK We are the same person. Of course we agree. Are you agreed?

RUTH I agree.

JACK We are a hell of a couple. Do you agree?

RUTH Agreed.

JACK And I will marry you. Agreed?

RUTH Agreed.

JACK You're not just saying that?

RUTH No, I agree!

JACK I agree too!

RUTH I agree with your agreement!

JACK So do we break open a bottle of bubbly and agree some more? Shall we effervesce till wedding bells wake us in the morning?

RUTH Effervesce? No, no. Let's fore*effer*vesce.

JACK Agreed! God, it's wonderful being agreeable. (*He goes into the kitchen and brings in an open bottle of champagne and two glasses. As he pours:*) Okay. I'm getting married. Not what I expected when I woke up this morning. Life took a bit of a zigzag there at the party, but what the hell. That's what parties are for. Agreed?

RUTH Oui.

JACK & RUTH (*Sing*) *"Oui, c'est elle! C'est la déesse plus charmante and plus belle!"*

JACK *"Oui, c'est elle! C'est la déesse qui descend parmi nous—"* (*Realizes that Ruth isn't singing anymore*) What's the matter, I'm pearl-fishing by myself here, suddenly.

RUTH You know, they'd have to be Jewish.

JACK Who. The sixty-five rabbis who are going to tie the kosher knot? They're Jewish already. I hope.

RUTH No, I mean, our kids. The little Jacks.

JACK The little Jacks will be Jewish. I believe.

RUTH But I mean—they'd have to be brought up Jewish.

JACK Which means—?

RUTH Brought up Jewish.

JACK They'd be Jewish anyway. Isn't that in Deuteronomy? Jewish genes pass through the mother? So what's the . . . ?

RUTH That's not what I mean.

JACK You mean—?

RUTH I mean I'd want my kids brought up the way I was. I wouldn't feel right if my kids didn't go to temple and Hebrew school and do everything I did.

JACK Wait a minute. *Hebrew school—*?

RUTH Hebrew school.

JACK Stop kidding around.

RUTH Who's kidding around?

JACK Hebrew school. What for?

RUTH To learn Hebrew.

JACK Yeah I know but—*what for*? Are there any great detective novels written in Hebrew? Besides the Bible, I mean?

RUTH I went to Hebrew school when I was a kid.

JACK I toasted cats over bonfires when I was a kid, but I wouldn't want my kids to do that.

Small pause.

RUTH You didn't *really* toast cats over bonfires . . . ?

JACK No, I didn't toast cats over fires. They were hamsters. *Small* hamsters. But I think you said . . .

RUTH Hebrew school.

JACK Hebrew school.

RUTH What's wrong with Hebrew school? Your grandmother was German and you—

JACK (*Under*) Great-grandmother.

RUTH —speak German. I'm Jewish and I'd want my kids to learn Hebrew. Maybe they'd want to wail at the wall in Jerusalem sometime.

JACK Do you really think that I could buy this?

RUTH   Well . . . You'd have to buy it, I mean . . .

JACK   What are you going to do? Are you going to tell your kids that there's a god? A Jewish god?

RUTH   I don't know what I'll tell them.

JACK   An Isaac Bashevis Singer in the sky?

RUTH   I don't know what I'll tell them. A Mel Brooks in the sky, but *some*body in the sky. Somebody or something *some*where, anyway.

JACK   You'll have to tell them something halfway believable. And don't you think you'd better think about it, before you have them?

RUTH   What would *you* tell our kids?

JACK   I'd tell them I don't know. I'd tell them to think about it.

RUTH   Well I couldn't do that.

JACK   So what do you do?

RUTH   You bring them up in a tradition and let them figure things out for themselves.

JACK   Oh. A tradition.

RUTH   That's right.

JACK   Sure. So they can produce more kids who pass that stuff on without thinking about it. You're a smart woman, Ruth! You're a modern adult!

RUTH   Kids can't just grow up with nothing.

JACK   But you don't believe any of that stuff!

RUTH   How do you know what I believe? You've never had any interest in what I believe.

JACK   Do you believe it? Jewish law? Pork is dirty? Saturday is sacred to the Lord?

RUTH   (*Overlapping, from "to the Lord"*)   This doesn't have anything to do with believing.

JACK   *Do you believe it*? If you don't believe it, then why bring your kids up that way? And if you do believe it, why aren't you in temple every week?

RUTH   Maybe I'm not a very good Jew. Maybe I'm a lousy Jew. Maybe I don't keep up with things as well as I should—

JACK   (*Overlapping her last words*)   So what are you going to pass on but lousy Jewishness? And you're not a Jew anyway. You're you, remember? You're Ruth.

RUTH   I'm afraid I am a Jew.

JACK   But that's just an *idea*!

RUTH   I am a Jew.

JACK   That's not what's important!

RUTH   What *is* important?

JACK   What you *are*.

RUTH   What I *am* is a Jew, and *that's* important.

JACK   (*Overlapping her words*)   What you *are* is important.

RUTH   (*Overlapping him*)   Deciding what you want out of life is important. And kids are important. And living in a tradition is important. Otherwise—

JACK   You're just hanging onto a tradition for the sake of hanging on to it!

RUTH   What's it to you if I hang onto the way I was brought up?

JACK   Just for the sake of hanging on to it?

RUTH   Yes. Maybe.

JACK   In your head you're still a twelve-year-old girl going to Hebrew school and believing what your parents tell you.

RUTH   Well I'm sorry, but I can't turn my back on five thousand years of human society the way you can. And I can't treat my parents like people I met on a bus, the way you can. And I can't live two thousand years in the future, in some utopia. And don't say, "What century is this?" because I don't care. And don't go into "superstition and slavery" because I've heard that speech a hundred thousand times. It doesn't matter what the world is *supposed* to be like. It's not like that. It's not utopia and it never will be. It's like *this,* and we have to live in it. And I want a husband and family to live in it with me.

JACK   One small problem here is that you want a husband but you don't seem to care who fills the position. You even invited a spare possibility to your party in case I didn't work out.

RUTH   I didn't invite him.

JACK   Before you'd even put the question to me.

RUTH   I didn't invite him.

JACK   Is Josh outside right now, listening at the keyhole? We can call him in here and you can pop the question to *him.* See if *Josh* works out.

RUTH   *I didn't invite him.*

JACK   At least I admit that I don't like marriage. Do you realize you've spent fifteen years steering clear of it?

RUTH I've never met a man I . . .

JACK Do you think it's some kind of *accident* you're not married now, with kids? Do you think that is happenstance, Ruth?

RUTH I've never met a man I wanted to marry before.

JACK No. You haven't been going out with men you *could* marry. Men your parents could accept.

RUTH Can we forget about my parents?

JACK Do you think that if they didn't come to your birthday party, they'd come to your wedding? To me? No fuckin' way, sweetheart! And you couldn't live with that. Because when it comes down to it, you are a good Jewish daughter. You're thirty-five years old and you won't tell your parents to just fuck off!

RUTH Have you ever thought that maybe you're just a bigot?

JACK Oh. A bigot.

RUTH That's the word.

JACK An anti-Semite. Is that what you're calling me?

RUTH Just like your lovely parents. In *their* great tradition.

JACK Yes. Bigots because of their *politeness*.

RUTH Maybe you don't want your kids brought up Jewish because you're a bigot.

JACK I don't want my kids brought up *anything*—

RUTH Maybe you don't like Esther because she's a Jew.

JACK I don't like Esther because she's trying to pry us apart.

RUTH When you start in on that fucking accent and telling those fucking jokes—

JACK (*Overlaps from "fucking jokes"*) I have heard that accent out of *your own mouth,* lady!

RUTH I can say those things. You can't!

JACK Oh yeah? How come you can insult the Germans and the French and anybody else, but your own goddamn tribe is so sacred?

RUTH (*From "your own tribe"*) Nobody ever tried to *exterminate* the Germans and the French. And maybe you're just a bigot.

JACK All right. We're getting down to definitions now. I'm an anti-Semitic parasite. And you, what are you? Let's see. How about "something indistinguishable from your good friend Esther." You want a house, you want a husband, you want your blue shoes—

RUTH (*Underneath his next words*) Will you shut up about those fucking shoes?

JACK You want, you want, you want. Why not just change your name to Trendstein and find yourself a sheikh?

RUTH I don't think that I'm being unreasonable—

JACK (*Underneath her words*) Marry into a toilet paper fortune.

RUTH —to ask for certain things out of a marriage.

JACK What are you, a fucking *JAP*?

Pause.

RUTH Okay. I want certain things from this world. And from a marriage. If that makes me a JAP—fine. I'm a JAP. I want a house and I want some kids who can enjoy what *I* enjoyed when I was a kid, which had much to do with being Jewish. Is that being a JAP? I don't think it's a crime to want a husband, or not to want to be poor in this world. Life is too short for being poor. And if you won't provide those things then I have to find someone who will.

JACK   Oh. "Provide" them for you . . .

RUTH   No, provide them *with* me. How long are you planning to live the life that *you* do? Without this and without that. When are you planning to grow up a little?

JACK   I have been living the life that I want to. On principles that I believe in.

RUTH   Well it's not the life that I want.

Silence.

JACK   So I guess we both have our answer.

Silence.

RUTH   You're always saying that what's important is likeness.

JACK   That is what's important.

RUTH   And being alike.

JACK   We *are* alike.

RUTH   Maybe we're not as alike as we thought.

JACK   Jesus Christ, we are the same person, Ruth. We are the *same person!*

RUTH   Sure we have fun together. Sure we laugh a lot and have a good time. Sure we fuck well together. Other people fuck well together. So what's so special about us?

JACK   How long have you been planning to dump me, Ruth?

RUTH   I don't believe that you would say that—

JACK   No no no. How long have you been planning to get rid of me? Since before Esther's cousin's anniversary thing, or after?

RUTH   You can be such an asshole.

JACK   And I thought I was so fucking smart! You didn't really *mean* it when you asked me to marry you!

RUTH   I did mean it.

JACK   That was just a *show*.

RUTH   I did mean it.

JACK   Well you did it very well. It was very convincing.

RUTH   (*Under his next words*)   I meant it!

JACK   Will you marry me, Jack, because if you won't then we can't be together anymore. Knowing all along what the answer was likely to be. You only asked me to marry you so that I could turn you down and you could drive me out!

RUTH   *All right then, leave!*

JACK   *Fuck you!*

RUTH   *Then leave!*

JACK   *Fuck you!*

RUTH   *Leave!*

JACK   *Fucking JAP!*

RUTH   *Will you leave?*

JACK   And the megabytes slew the corned beef hashemites and the overbites destroyed the philobytes because they worshipped a different god!

RUTH   Will you stop this? Will you stop? Make it stop. Make it stop. Make it stop.

RUTH Make it stop.

JACK Okay well I guess this is it, huh. Any way I cut it I can't win here. Any answer I give you—yes, no—it's the wrong answer. Or am I wrong? Are we over? Are we done?

RUTH I think we are.

JACK So we're through.

RUTH I think we are.

JACK Just like that.

RUTH So what do we do, Jack?

JACK Well Esther is bound to be delighted by this turn of events.

RUTH Could you please not bring Esther into this—

JACK I can just see it. She'll be going around to everyone and saying, "It was his fault, you know. It was *his fault.*" And I won't even be there to call her an asshole. The triumph of the utterly mediocre.

RUTH Jack, if we have to come to a stop, can't we find some civilized way to do it . . .

JACK "Civilized" . . . No, I'll tell you how we do it. If this is over then that means it's over, pal. Over. You know? Over? That means that after I walk out that door—as I will very shortly—then I don't want to see you, I don't want to hear from you, I don't want you to write me, or call me—I don't even want you to think about me. I don't even want you to *remember* me. You are history, pal. You are erased. You died today.

RUTH Don't say that—

JACK (*Overlapping her*) If this is over, then this is gone.

RUTH   You don't really mean that.

JACK   *You are tearing the heart right out of me!* And then you say that I don't *mean* it? Oh Jesus! Jesus . . . !

The phone rings loudly, once. "Au fond du temple saint" fades up, then fades away.

RUTH   So what do we do, Jack? What do we do?

JACK   I don't know.

RUTH   How do we stop?

JACK   I have no idea.

RUTH   Two people who are the same person who are crazy about each other.

JACK   I have no idea.

RUTH   Maybe we could have some kind of a timetable. You know—cut down on each other the way people quit smoking.

JACK   Sure. Instead of Smoke Enders—

RUTH   Joke Enders.

JACK   First one phone call a day, then a phone call every other day—see each other a little less, till we're just a crack of light under the door.

RUTH   And then we vanish.

JACK   Exactly. I mean, take the long view. Does it really matter if two schmucks in some obscure corner of the universe move off in different directions? Will the cosmos tremble?

RUTH   Nope.

JACK   Not a hair. So what's the big . . . Jesus, Ruth. I can't even look at you. (*Puts a hand over his heart*)   And where are those braille pajamas when you really need them. To tell you where you are.

RUTH   I'm sorry, Jack.

JACK   Don't be sorry.

RUTH   I'm sorry anyway. I feel sorry.

JACK   I just can't imagine it. I'm spoiled. I can't imagine life without you. No Ruth? I'd be a half of something.

RUTH   I'll tell you what you'd be.

JACK   What.

RUTH   You know what you'd be?

JACK   What.

RUTH   Ruth-less.

JACK   Ouch. Ouch.

RUTH   You know, the sad thing . . . The really sad thing isn't that things come to an end. Or that people go out of your life or die. The really sad thing about the world is that you get over it.

JACK   I won't get over it.

RUTH   And you forget what really happened and how things were.

JACK   I won't forget.

RUTH   You forget who said what.

JACK   I won't forget.

RUTH You forget how happy you were.

JACK I won't forget.

RUTH Six months from now, we'll be ancient history.

JACK Hell isn't other people. Hell is remembering other people. Getting them stuck in your memory. Playing things over and over and over again, like a piece of music you can't get out of your head.

The climax of "Oui c'est elle" comes on.

RUTH Hold me, Jack. Hold onto me. Make it stop.

He does. The scene looks just as it did at the start of the play, with them in each other's arms. Slowly, they begin to dance.

RUTH Paradise.

JACK Absolutely. *Dip.*

They dip.

RUTH This is what I call *shayn.*

JACK Me too. What's a *"shayn"*?

RUTH *Shayn* is an ancient Yiddish word, for "pretty damn nifty."

JACK Ah-ha. *"Shayn!* Come back!"

RUTH *Dip.* Pinky—what do you say we never stop.

JACK Pinky—it's a deal.

RUTH So are we setting up for this party, or are we dancing?

JACK We're dancing. Obviously.

RUTH Oh, right. So we are.

JACK   And it's paradise.

RUTH & JACK   Dip.

JACK   Do you realize what the world would be like if everybody lived like this?

RUTH   Would it be utopia?

JACK   There'd be no war. No hatred. No hunger. No strife.

RUTH   But will it ever stop?

JACK   It'd be heaven on earth.

RUTH   Jack, will we ever stop?

JACK   No polyester. No parents . . .

RUTH   Jack . . .

JACK   It's paradise.

RUTH   Will we ever stop?

They dance. The lights fade until there is only a crack of light under the door. Then that is gone.

END OF PLAY

DON JUAN
IN CHICAGO

This play is for Casey Childs

Don Juan in Chicago premiered in New York City in March 1995, at Primary Stages (Casey Childs, artistic director). The play was directed by Robert Stanton; sets were by Bob Phillips; lighting was by Deborah Constantine; costumes were by Jennifer von Mayrhauser; music and sound design were by David van Tieghem; props were by Deirdre Brennan; fight direction was by B. H. Barry; and the production stage manager was Christine Catti. The cast was as follows:

DON JUAN	Simon Brooking
LEPORELLO	Larry Block
MEPHISTOPHELES	Peter Bartlett
DONA ELVIRA	J. Smith-Cameron
SANDY	Nancy Opel
TODD	T. Scott Cunningham
MIKE	Mark Setlock
ZOEY	Dina Spybey

ACT I

Seville, 1599. Lightning and thunder as lights come up on a chamber in Don Juan's palace: a door to the outside, a door to the rest of the palace, and a window up right.

DON JUAN—*thirty, handsome, wearing a severe black doublet and ruff—is mixing a blood-red liquid from a recipe in an enormous ancient tome. Bubbling alchemical flasks. A skull. A pentagram drawn on the floor. A wall of books.*

DON JUAN   Sanguis melanchrys bovis atque caput avis, incipite! Lingua serpentis et folium floris, commiscite!
  (*"Golden black blood of an ox and head of a bird, begin! Tongue of serpent and leaf of flower, mix together!"*)

Louder lightning and thunder.

LEPORELLO (*O.S.*)   Don Juan! Hello? (LEPORELLO *enters with a food tray.*)   Don Juan, it's the end of the world out there today!

DON JUAN   It's not the end, Leporello. It's the beginning!

LEPORELLO   Oh, forsooth? Well, a big red cloud just poured out ashes, burning sulfur, and snakes.

DON JUAN   Excellent.

LEPORELLO   And the ashes and the snakes—they fell only on *this palace,* Don Juan.

DON JUAN   I'll bet they did.

LEPORELLO   The rest of Seville? Brilliant sunshine! Here? We got reptiles blowing in the windows!

DON JUAN (*Consults book*)   "One speck of twilight, one virgin's tear, set hourglass to five minutes and let simmer."

LEPORELLO   Question, master: This little alchemistry set here—this didn't have anything to do with today's reptilian drizzle . . . ?

DON   I'm calling up Satan.

LEPORELLO   Oh, is *that* what's up? The Prince of Darkness is dropping by?

DON   Hence the ashes and the snakes. (*Intoning over his alchemical mixture*)   Eeee-yong! Wonga wonga wonga wonga!

LEPORELLO   My prince, how old are you these days?

DON JUAN   Twenty-nine. No—thirty, now.

LEPORELLO   Happy birthday. So you're thirty, you're rich, you also still have your virginity.

DON JUAN   As far as I know.

LEPORELLO   Mi amigo, the world is your cloister. Why don't you pay your debt to biology and get yourself a girlfriend.

DON JUAN   Life is too short for that.

LEPORELLO   No, life is short so gather ye gonads while ye may!

DON JUAN   I just don't see the point of carnal relations.

LEPORELLO   Will you look around you, señor? (*Don Juan looks around himself.*)   No, I mean get outa this room and *then* look around—what are you gonna see? *People—shtupping—everywhere.*

DON JUAN   Not in public—?

LEPORELLO No, not in public but showing up in public with silly grins on their faces. Women with this *glow,* have you seen that? Night and day, man and beast are engaged in this strange activity. And why?

DON JUAN I guess it's a mystery.

LEPORELLO Because it's *wonderful.* I babysit you twenty-nine hours a day, I still find time to dip my strawberry.

DON JUAN I don't know where.

LEPORELLO In the scullery, with Allison the milkmaid. Oh God, sweet Allison the milkmaid! And you sit here while such goddesses walk the streets? Wake up and smell the pollen! Did you notice the babe in the third row, by the way?

DON JUAN Yes. Very pretty.

LEPORELLO (*Waving into audience*) Hiya, honey!

DON JUAN (*To woman in audience*) I apologize for my servant, señora.

LEPORELLO Look at her, Don, look!

DON JUAN Yes, yes, very attractive. But to go through all the work of locating a woman and then pursuing her?

LEPORELLO What work? You're Don Juan de Tenorio! You don't have to pursue! They'll locate *you!* Doña Elvira walks by here twenty times a day. (*Pronounced "El-VEER-a"*) Batting the lashes. Fanning, fanning.

DON JUAN So many women are only interested in clothing, and jewelry . . .

LEPORELLO Hey. This is the sixteenth century. Women don't have any *outlets.*

DON JUAN They don't?

LEPORELLO No. They're repressed by bastards like us!

DON JUAN So it's a social issue.

LEPORELLO Help womankind, my magnanimous master. Locate a person of the female persuasion. Talk about Plato with her, instead of with me, who doesn't give a shit. Realize her potential. And sleep with her twice a night. It's a great deal! Totally symbiotic!

DON JUAN (*Holds up the skull*) Do you know what this is?

LEPORELLO The sickest paperweight in Seville.

DON JUAN This was once a man like you.

LEPORELLO Better paid, I bet. So what are we supposed to do, bury ourselves alive?

DON JUAN Do you know what's truly important in this world?

LEPORELLO Fellatio?

DON JUAN Knowledge.

LEPORELLO You're a *freak*. And will ya give me a raise, please?

DON JUAN You just got one.

LEPORELLO Eighteen years ago.

A flash of lightning outside.

DON JUAN The sands have run out. You have to go.

LEPORELLO Oh, sure. I talk wages, suddenly the *boogey man* is dropping by.

Ominous rumbling and a chorus of mystical voices. More lightning and thunder.

DON JUAN   Leave, Leporello! *Go!*

LEPORELLO   And turn off the snakes!

Leporello exits. Don Juan stands in the pentagram.

DON JUAN   *In nomine omnium nefariorum imperiorum, coniuro te!*
Appareat Mephistophilis!
(*"In the name of all the impious empires I conjure you! Appear,*
Mephistopheles!")

The storm climaxes, and in a puff of smoke, MEPHISTOPHELES
appears. A cosmopolitan fellow.

DON JUAN   Are you—Lord Mephistopheles . . . ?

MEPHISTOPHELES   At your worship's service, if you please.

DON JUAN   Keep off, Satan! Avaunt!
Thou canst not touch me in this pentagram!

MEPHISTOPHELES   I'm sorry. Is this Seville, or Amsterdam?

DON JUAN   (*Spanish: "Seh-VEE-ah"*)   Sevilla.

MEPHISTOPHELES   You did call me, I believe.

DON JUAN   That was the idea.

MEPHISTOPHELES   Thank—I won't say God—I'm relieved.
I hate arriving at the wrong door.

DON JUAN   I've never called up a phantasma before!
(*Mephistopheles coughs.*)   Are you all right . . . ?

MEPHISTOPHELES   Asthma. (*Cough*)   What a bore.
The smoke can make these entrances rough.
What's the local time, just off the cuff?

DON JUAN   May 1599. No—June.

MEPHISTOPHELES   Ah-ha. Morning?

Don Juan in Chicago

DON JUAN	Afternoon—I think. But can I offer you something to drink? A glass?
MEPHISTOPHELES	Alas. Such pleasures are inaccessible In my *milieu*.
DON JUAN	And yet you have asthma?
MEPHISTOPHELES	*I* can't explain it. Can *yieu*?
DON JUAN	You did revolt against the king of heaven.
MEPHISTOPHELES	A complicated story. (*Notices the skull*) Eiuw.
DON JUAN	Oh that. A paperweight of mine. Maybe sort of foolish.
MEPHISTOPHELES	Not to mention sort of . . .
DON JUAN	Ghoulish?
MEPHISTOPHELES	But to tell you true, Don Juan, I'm shocked to hear from such a paragon. A man with everything from gold to great ability. A man who even has his original virginity?
DON JUAN	Yes, that's still intact.
MEPHISTOPHELES	Hasn't been sacked yet? Is that a fact . . . And I'm here to dicker for your soul?
DON JUAN	If you don't snicker at the role.
MEPHISTOPHELES	*Enchanté.*
DON JUAN	And if I can.

MEPHISTOPHELES   I'm honored to deal with such a man.
For tinkers and tailors, cabbies and kings,
People sell souls for the stupidest things.
Trinkets and trifles—
You name it, they'll ask it.
This world is going to hell not *in,*
But *for* a handbasket.
But I'm off the track. Please excuse me.
You Who Have Everything—pray,
How can you use me?

DON JUAN   It's true, as you say, that I have lots.

MEPHISTOPHELES   Unlimited money.

DON   I have pots!
Yet I lack one crucial dimension.

MEPHISTOPHELES   The tension
Is killing, but let me guess.
Is it something invisible?

DON JUAN   Yes. It's everyone's greatest hope.

MEPHISTOPHELES   You want to be pope.

DON JUAN   Nope.

MEPHISTOPHELES   Sorry. A personal kink.
But wait a second, let me think . . .

DON JUAN   I know you're going to chortle.

MEPHISTOPHELES   Cross my heart.

DON JUAN   I want to be immortal.
I know it's a bit much.

MEPHISTOPHELES   No, no, not as such.
But despite what you hear

I can't turn you into Dante
Or—who's that lunkhead? Shakespeare.
But please, *persévérer*.

DON JUAN
I mean I want to live forever.
Here I am twenty-nine—no, thirty,
Middle age is brewing,
And I haven't done a thing worth doing.
Three decades and nothing to show for it!
Why *shouldn't* I sell my soul?

MEPHISTOPHELES
Go for it.

DON JUAN
With unlimited minutes
I could discover the meaning of life!
The eternal truths of time,
What the basis of the cosmos is!
If not by study, then—

MEPHISTOPHELES
By osmosis.

DON JUAN
I could become a household name!
"Don Juan" could be a synonym for brain!

MEPHISTOPHELES
Unless some other organ brings you fame . . .
Well, I don't want to trick you, but
I think I can fix you. I mean, fix you up.
Though it wouldn't be free.
There is a quid pro quo.

DON JUAN
You mean my soul?

MEPHISTOPHELES
The traditional fee.

DON JUAN
But that's where my plan's so slick!
You want me to gamble my soul
And I'll willingly bet it.
If I live forever, you'll never get it!

MEPHISTOPHELES	(*Magically producing a parchment*) Technically.
DON JUAN	A contract, already?
MEPHISTOPHELES	These things are boilerplate. Standard as hymns.
DON JUAN	"DAMNATION AGREEMENT."
MEPHISTOPHELES	I know it sounds grim. Just date it and sign where it says . . .
DON JUAN	"Victim"?

Leporello enters.

LEPORELLO	Hey, Don Juan! Did el Diablo ever find you?
DON JUAN	Actually, he's standing right behind you.
LEPORELLO	Oooh, I'm shaking. I'm *jello*. Maybe His Darkness would like a liqueur, Or a bubbly with lime?
DON JUAN	Leporello, could you come back another time?
LEPORELLO	Oh sure! The hell am I doing talking in rhyme . . . ?
DON JUAN	Maybe later, since we're secluded? I want to get the work in hand . . .
LEPORELLO	Concluded. I understand. (*To audience*) This guy is deluded! He's a psychopath! (*Starts out*) Adios, Mephisto! Blow it out your ath!

Leporello exits.

DON JUAN	Sorry about that. He's not malicious.
MEPHISTOPHELES	*No problemo.* I find him . . . delicious.
DON JUAN	But you said you might get my soul. Can you give me a hint?
MEPHISTOPHELES	It's hard to explain—
DON JUAN	What's this small print? "Don Juan must seduce A different woman *every day*"?!
MEPHISTOPHELES	One by every midnight, Or I come and take you away.
DON JUAN	To hell?
MEPHISTOPHELES	Oh pshaw, man! It's a straw man! A formality! And regular sex is a pittance To pay for immortality. Pricks one's interest, wouldn't you say?
DON JUAN	But a different woman every day?
MEPHISTOPHELES	And no woman twice. That's the sum of it.
DON JUAN	Sort of challenging.
MEPHISTOPHELES	That's the fun of it! Get the knack, it's easy as pie.
DON JUAN	But I've never seduced, past or present.
MEPHISTOPHELES	Just get down on your knees and lie. I hear it's quite pleasant. Meantime, you'll be on the scent Of the meaning of life. You'll be a terrier! As for these women, to quote the cliché—

DON JUAN	The more the merrier.
MEPHISTOPHELES	Touché.
	You're after the biggest of game, Don Juan!
	Who cares if you have to *chercher la femme*?
DON JUAN	I could always pay a woman to agree.
MEPHISTOPHELES	Clause 22. The sex must be free.
	(*Rolling up the contract*) But if you don't want to sign,
	I can't force you to it.
DON JUAN	No, no. Let's do it.
MEPHISTOPHELES	A more generous offer could not be made.
DON JUAN	Do I have to sign in blood?
MEPHISTOPHELES	Tradition, I'm afraid.
	An enigma—like my asthma.
	So pick a digit and let's draw plasma.
DON JUAN	What about Leporello, my hired man?
	I'll need a fellow
	To keep things spic and span.
MEPHISTOPHELES	We could write him in—
	Make him immortal too.
DON JUAN	Without his consent?
MEPHISTOPHELES	He's just a servant.
DON JUAN	It's true.

Mephistopheles runs a quill across Don Juan's finger, drawing blood, and hands him the quill to dip in it.

MEPHISTOPHELES	Sign away and be my guest.

DON JUAN   (*Signing*)   *Finito! Consummatum est!*

MEPHISTOPHELES   Congratulations! Well done!

DON JUAN   So when does eternity begin?

MEPHISTOPHELES   Oh it's begun, my metaphysical gambler.
                    You're fixed now like a fly in amber.

DON JUAN   I don't feel any change.

MEPHISTOPHELES   You never will. You'll never age
                    While the universe moves faster and faster.

DON JUAN   I don't know how to thank you.

MEPHISTOPHELES   Oh, don't thank me. Just call me master.
(*A thunderclap. "Receive, O Hades, your king! Take
Mephistopheles!":*)   *Recipe, O Tantare, tuum regem! Accipe
Mephistophelem!*

Mephistopheles disappears. Storm subsides.

DON JUAN   So I'm immortal. I'm going to live forever! What
now? *Leporello!*

Leporello enters.

LEPORELLO   My liege? How was your visit with "Satan"?

DON JUAN   Wonderful.

LEPORELLO   Something burning in here . . . ?

DON JUAN   Leporello, I have to find a woman.

LEPORELLO   Well, it's about time! Congratulations! (*Pumps the
Don's hand*)   Oh, is that a hard-on? I beg your pard-on.

DON JUAN   One woman by midnight tonight and another
tomorrow.

LEPORELLO Wow. Really going for it, huh. Well you gotta be dying of terminal horniness by now.

DON JUAN But that's just it! I'm not dying of *anything*. And neither are you! HA HA HA HA! We . . . are not dying . . . of *ANYTHING*!

LEPORELLO You seem demented, my prince.

DON JUAN Well why not? *WE'RE NOT DYING ANYMORE!*

LEPORELLO Uh-huh. Well, we'll find you a real honey.

DON JUAN She needn't be a honey. I can give her about three minutes, as soon as possible.

LEPORELLO Padrone. This is your first time. Wouldn't you like it to be sort of a beautiful experience? Or would you settle for a toothless one-eyed hunchback.

DON JUAN Yes. Fine. Anything.

LEPORELLO Lemme see what I can scrape up. (*Gothic doorbell*) But hark. A caller?

DON JUAN I can't see anyone until I've had a woman.

LEPORELLO (*Looking out the window*) But this is heaven-sent! It's Doña Elvira, all oiled and perfumed. The mountain has come to jump on Mohammed!

DON JUAN Let her in. But Leporello?

LEPORELLO Yes, my amorous one?

DON JUAN What do I say?

LEPORELLO Oh, the usual eternal sentiments. How beautiful she is, how you got carried away, you lay awake at night and burn for her . . .

DON JUAN I'd better write this down. (*Scribbles on the palm of his hand*) "Beautiful. Carried away. Lie awake . . ."

LEPORELLO Burn.

DON JUAN "Burn for her . . ."

LEPORELLO She's a goddess.

DON JUAN "Goddess . . ."

LEPORELLO You're an idiot.

DON JUAN "Idiot . . ."

LEPORELLO Scratch that out. Did you cut your finger?

DON JUAN Yes, I wanted to talk about that . . .

LEPORELLO Women also like getting called stuff like dove, pigeon.

DON JUAN "Dove. Pigeon . . ."

LEPORELLO Think pet shop.

DON JUAN "Pet shop . . ."

Gothic doorbell.

LEPORELLO She ain't gonna wait forever.

DON JUAN By the way, Leporello. You're immortal now.

LEPORELLO Oh, great. Excuse me?

DON JUAN You're going to live forever. So am I.

LEPORELLO Forsooth?

DON JUAN I made a deal that gave us eternal life.

LEPORELLO Ah-ha. Does eternal life include a raise?

DON JUAN You'd better let Doña Elvira in.

LEPORELLO Wait, wait, wait. You made a deal.

DON JUAN We live forever. (*Takes a dagger and stabs Leporello in the chest*) You see? Nothing can kill us as long as I stay lucky.

LEPORELLO Interesting. Question B.—You can stop now.— What does "luck" have to do with this? And I sense this is the nitty-gritty, so help me out.

DON JUAN I have to sleep with a woman a day.

LEPORELLO Or? You mean sulfur and brimstone? The terminal tan? And I was somehow involved in this transaction?

DON JUAN I signed for you.

LEPORELLO Oh *good*. So you wrote me into a contract with Satan under which you, who have never seduced even a sheep in your whole miserable life, now have to soften up a woman a *day*? YOU FUCKING MORON! YOU CRETIN!

DON JUAN Watch yourself.

LEPORELLO What're you gonna do? *Kill* me?

DON JUAN I can't.

LEPORELLO And you never thought, "*Whoa,* Leporello might have some input"?

DON JUAN You're only a servant.

LEPORELLO So why wait? Toss me on the barbie right now! And there I was flipping Satan the bird. (*Babbling*) Help me, God, help me, help me!

DON JUAN I don't think he can.

LEPORELLO So Elvira has to be *in the mood*? It's either come, or kingdom come?

DON JUAN At least through tomorrow.

LEPORELLO Why don't you tell her, "Oh by the way. If you don't sleep with me, I go to hell for all eternity." That's *novel*. See if you score.

DON JUAN Do you think she'd believe me?

LEPORELLO Y'see, it all depends on the foreplay.

DON JUAN "Foreplay" . . . ?

LEPORELLO I'll go let her in.

Leporello exits.

DON JUAN (*Checks the palm of his hand*) "Beautiful. Carried away. Burning goddess." Burning goddess?

Leporello enters.

LEPORELLO Doña Elvira! And God bless us, every one!

DOÑA ELVIRA *sweeps in, with fan, and Leporello exits.*

DON JUAN Doña Elvira.

ELVIRA Don Juan! Thank God you're safe!
You and your vassal.

DON JUAN Why shouldn't I be safe?

ELVIRA Well, snakes were falling on your castle.

DON JUAN Ah, that. I'm sorry if they misgave you.

ELVIRA I thought I might drop by and save you.
Excuse me for barging in like this,
Unannounced and unchaperoned.

DON JUAN   No, please.

ELVIRA   Having sent my duenna on a trip to Ravenna
             To buy some cologne.

DON JUAN   It's fine.

ELVIRA   What I mean is, we're quite, quite *alone*.

DON JUAN   I fully understand.

ELVIRA   You know you *might* kiss my hand. (*She holds out
             her hand. He kisses it. She forces him to his knees.*)
             Oh no, please don't kneel.

DON JUAN   (*Starting to rise*)   Very well.

ELVIRA   (*Forcing him back down*)   But I know how you feel.

DON JUAN   Excuse me?

ELVIRA   Passion blurs the way we should steer
             When we are ruled by desire and—what?

DON JUAN   Fear?

ELVIRA   I see you understand.

DON JUAN   I don't think I do . . .

ELVIRA   So you feel it too?

DON JUAN   Feel what?

He starts to rise, but she forces him back down.

ELVIRA   Not yet. Be still.
             Just let me drink my fill
             And then be gone, my Giovanni.

DON JUAN   But . . .

ELVIRA   My Svengali.

DON JUAN   I was hoping you'd stay.

ELVIRA   No, truly, I must go away.
            In my heart of hearts I've already sinned
            Coming here and throwing caution to the wind.

DON JUAN   I don't think I . . .

ELVIRA   Oh, my savior!
            I know this is peculiar behavior
            From a woman you hardly know.

DON JUAN   We did speak once.

ELVIRA   My heart was too full to say what I mean.

DON JUAN   I think it was near the city latrine.

ELVIRA   You remember!
            Oh I was faint! I was on fire!

DON JUAN   Because of the odor?

ELVIRA   Because of *desire*.
            You're on guard against your passion, I see.
            Oh my angel, you're so much better than me!
            Your soul is like the uppermost fruit
            On the highest bough.

DON JUAN   May I get up now?

ELVIRA   Unreachable. Unimpeachable.
            Can I make it any clearer?
            Don Juan?

DON JUAN   Yes, Doña Elvira?

ELVIRA   I'm pouring out my suit
            Yet you don't have much to say.

DON JUAN   I'm sorry. I guess I just got . . . (*Happens to glance at his hand*)
"Carried away."

ELVIRA   Carried away? Yes, by—?

DON JUAN   (*Checks hand*)   Your beauty?

ELVIRA   *Continuez.*

DON JUAN   (*Reading from his hand*)   I lie inert . . . all night
. . . bumming for you.

ELVIRA   "Inert" and "bumming"?

DON JUAN   Or alert and beaming.

ELVIRA   It's possible.

DON JUAN   Flossing and squirming?

ELVIRA   (*Checking his palm for him*)   Oh. "*Burning.*"

DON JUAN   Yes, burning for you.

ELVIRA   You don't.

DON JUAN   I do. (*Checks hand*)   "My godless idiot." Or
"gormless."

ELVIRA   (*Checks hand*)   That is what it looks like.

DON JUAN   Sort of formless.

ELVIRA   Is that more down here on the wrist?

DON JUAN   A birthmark.

ELVIRA   No matter. I get the gist.
(*Embraces him*)   Oh my precious,
I dreamed it would happen like this!

DON JUAN   You did?

ELVIRA   What absolute bliss!
But maybe it's time for . . . a . . . ?

DON JUAN   Kiss?

ELVIRA   My Adonis!

They kiss, as Leporello enters.

LEPORELLO   Hiya, boys and girls! It's only me, the humble proletarian, airing out this old mattress here. (*He unfolds a bed from the wall.*)   Now how's that for a pleasant stretch of ticking? (*To audience*)   Whaddya think, folks? Will he get his nozzle off? (*To Don Juan and Elvira*)   Carry on, kids! *Mazeltov!*

Leporello hides behind the bed and observes.

ELVIRA   Well Don Juan, now that you're mine . . .

DON JUAN   Excuse me, do you have the time?

ELVIRA   I beg your pardon?

DON JUAN   Have you a watch of some kind?

ELVIRA   Really, Don Juan.

DON JUAN   You know these personal tics.

ELVIRA   Slightly unromantic, but—(*Checks watch*)—A quarter to six.

DON JUAN   Good, we're not running late.

ELVIRA   Do you have some appointment, or a date?

LEPORELLO   Romance her! Get to the sex!

DON JUAN   Actually—is it my answer?
I'm not sure what comes next.

Don Juan in Chicago

ELVIRA   Now that you and I have spoken . . .

DON JUAN   Would you like to lie down?

ELVIRA   Saucy boy! You give me a *token*.

DON JUAN   Sorry. I'm a little dull.

ELVIRA   Just any old token'll do.

DON JUAN   (*Holding it up*)   I do have a skull.

ELVIRA   How very kind.

DON JUAN   Inapropos?

ELVIRA   Not if it's *your* skull, my beau. (*Puts the skull back*)
            A toy or a trifle—any handy thing.
            Some family bauble. A *ring* . . .
            Maybe a gem to keep with me.

DON JUAN   Listen, if I give you something—
            Will you sleep with me?

ELVIRA   I *beg* your pardon, sir?!

DON JUAN   Was that a gaff?

LEPORELLO   Moron.

ELVIRA   Oh, I really have to laugh!
            I come to your door
            To be treated like some contemptible . . .

DON JUAN   Whore?

LEPORELLO   He had to say it.

ELVIRA   You wretch! You monster! You worm!

DON JUAN   I thought you couldn't think of the term!

ELVIRA   Oh, I see. Now the problem is *me*.

DON JUAN	Well, isn't it?
LEPORELLO	Go ahead. Insult her.
DON JUAN	Isn't that what you came here for? Adultery?
ELVIRA	We're not married, we can't commit adultery!
DON JUAN	Don't quibble with me!
ELVIRA	An impossibility, Given your command of the word!
DON JUAN	Sophist!
ELVIRA	Sophomore!
DON JUAN	Temptress!
ELVIRA	Turd!
DON JUAN	Now I see it! You came here to seduce me! I swear women were put on earth to test us.
LEPORELLO	Oh God, where's the asbestos?
DON JUAN	Will you defend your actions?
ELVIRA	I will if you'll let me.
LEPORELLO	Beelzebub? Come 'n' get me!
DON JUAN	Acquit yourself. You can, I trust.
ELVIRA	It's true I may have come here with lust In my heart . . .
DON JUAN	HA!
ELVIRA	But love was there too. Love was the greater part. Love, Don Juan, the greatest of the arts

That God, all-seeing,
Has given us: the uninstructed skill
Of cherishing another human being.
For I have loved you since the first day
I saw you at Mass in Seville.
I lived in hope, that's the sum of it.
When nothing seemed to come of it,
I took things into my own hands.
Oh I see too well you don't understand.
I'm sorry, Don Juan. Good-bye.

DON JUAN Elvira, if you don't sleep with me, I'll die!

Elvira stops at the door.

ELVIRA *Pardon?*

DON JUAN For all eternity I'll burn in the fiery pit.

ELVIRA Really?

LEPORELLO I think he may've hit it!

DON JUAN I'll languish in an everlasting prison.
Unto ages and ages I'll perish, my—(*Checks his hand*)
—Pigeon. My servant will, too.

ELVIRA I don't see what he's got to do with it.

DON JUAN You know how I cherish you.

ELVIRA Not really. Tell me.

DON JUAN How could you doubt me?

ELVIRA Give me *details*. What do you cherish about me?

DON JUAN Well . . .

LEPORELLO Praise her eyes!

DON JUAN	There's your size.
ELVIRA	My *size*?
DON JUAN	I mean—your eyes.
ELVIRA	Which I'm told are divine.
DON JUAN	And then there's your . . .
LEPORELLO	Hair.
DON JUAN	Your hair, which is . . .
ELVIRA	Top of the line.
LEPORELLO	Your lips.
DON JUAN	Your hips. Your bodice. Elvira, you're an absolute goddess!
LEPORELLO	How you suffer.
DON JUAN	How I suffer.
LEPORELLO	You love her!
DON JUAN	I love her!
ELVIRA	You love her *who*?
DON JUAN	Who else—(*Checks his hand*) —My pet shop—but you? I didn't know how to tell you. But now that I smell you— I mean, smell your perfume— And feel you so close . . .
ELVIRA	Resume.
DON JUAN	I don't know what to do!

ELVIRA   Then to our own selves let's be true.
                We're fated to be lovers, my treasure,
                Shouldn't we enjoy the ultimate pleasure
                If the heart is one and the blood is furious?

DON JUAN   I am getting rather curious . . .

ELVIRA   The merging of self at the urge of the flesh,
                The absolute rush, the intimate mesh?

DON JUAN   Yesh! Yesh! Yesh!

ELVIRA   And if you use your head
                There's only one place for it, darling.

DON JUAN   You mean . . . ?

LEPORELLO   Bed!

DON JUAN   Bed?

ELVIRA   Bed.

Don Juan and Elvira get into bed.

LEPORELLO   (*To audience, drawing the bed curtains*)   Okay, that's
enough! Pardon me while I veil this tender scene. We got
some theatrical voyeurs here, these guys who buy front-row
seats for the astronomical view of the ladies. I'm talking to
you, sicko. Anyway—
                So much for our intellectual hero.
                Copulation, one. Eternal truth, zero.
                I call it peachy.
                But hang on now . . . Steady . . .

DON   (*Orgasm, behind the curtain*)   Veni! *Vidi*! *VICI*!

LEPORELLO   Sounds like they're finished.
                The Don is done already . . . ?

The Don appears from the bed, bedraggled.

DON JUAN So that was sex. Well, well.

LEPORELLO And what's the verdict, my winsome gigolo?

DON JUAN (*Starts for the bed again*) Scientifically? I think it's worth a second try.

LEPORELLO Hold it, hold it! You can't, remember? She's off the list.

DON JUAN But Leporello, when I embraced her my heart leapt up. The feeling was ineffable!

LEPORELLO The problem is, your exes aren't eff-able.

ELVIRA (*From the bed*) Don Juan?

LEPORELLO I'm gone.

Leporello exits.

ELVIRA Don Juan? Hello? (*Looks out from the bed*) Hey there lover, where'd you go?

DON JUAN I'm sorry. Is there more?

ELVIRA More?

DON JUAN Somehow I thought that we were done.

ELVIRA In a manner of speaking. I lost. You won.

DON JUAN Amazing how short a time it took. But I was going to go back to my—

ELVIRA —Book? (*Slams it shut*) How dare you, sir!

DON JUAN You seem to be upset.

ELVIRA   I bare my body and this is what I get?
            Didn't you pledge your love?
            Offer me a token?

DON JUAN   The problem is—my dove—
            I'm already bespoken.

ELVIRA   You mean there's another woman?

DON JUAN   The thought is profane.

ELVIRA   Not a *man*?

DON JUAN   It's hard to explain.

ELVIRA   Oh *please*.
            Now that we've christened your couch.

DON JUAN   The long and short—

ELVIRA   I've had the short. Just give me the long.

DON JUAN   Ouch!
            We can't do this ever again.
            You see, I have this obligation . . .

ELVIRA   Oh. "Obligation." That's good.

DON JUAN   Which I'd undo if I could.

ELVIRA   Tell me a new one, Don Joo-un.

DON JUAN   Elvira, in matters of the heart
            Your experience is very varied.

ELVIRA   I had none till you.
            So we're very married.

DON JUAN   Alas, Elvira, that can never be.

ELVIRA   Never? That's your word?

DON JUAN	I have spoken. We must part.
ELVIRA	I gave you my heart and now it's broken. All these years there was the great Don Juan. Noble. Gracious. A sine qua non! Nothing was dearer to me than you.
DON JUAN	Forgive me, lady, if you can. Adieu.

Don Juan kisses her hand, and exits.

ELVIRA	Ravished and abandoned! Scorned and smeared! And am I, Doña Maria Elvira de Flores, Reduced to vulgar tears, A sobbing chorus? To be degraded by this oaf, this ox, Who turns the key and then discards the box? No! As God is my witness, by this hand, I will not rest until I have that man! Listen, you stars! Hear what I tell you!

In a puff of smoke, Mephistopheles appears.

MEPHISTOPHELES	Good evening. (*Cough*) Maybe I can help you.
ELVIRA	Who are you? A spirit? From what region? Don't tell me. Is your name . . . ?
MEPHISTOPHELES	Legion. It's true. But more importantly, Don Juan . . .
ELVIRA	Don't say that name, please, don't go on. Yes? Yes? Don Juan?
MEPHISTOPHELES	Do I see tears?
ELVIRA	I've burned for him for twenty years.

MEPHISTOPHELES	Well you know the adage: It's not the fire, it's the water damage.

He magically produces a handkerchief.

ELVIRA	Oh to catch him ere my hour chimes!
MEPHISTOPHELES	That might take a good long time.
ELVIRA	To have him just once more.
MEPHISTOPHELES	(*Magically producing a parchment*) Why don't you look at Paragraph 4.
ELVIRA	(*Reads*) "Doña Elvira . . ."
MEPHISTOPHELES	"Will never die . . ."
ELVIRA	"Till she and Don Juan . . ."
MEPHISTOPHELES	"A second time together lie." If you want a chance at him . . .
ELVIRA	A chance to dance in revenge on him. The slime. To grind in my heel!
MEPHISTOPHELES	The solution, my dear, is sublime. (*Produces the quill pen*) Let's make a deal.

Blackout.

Scene Two

Chicago. The present. Evening. Don's apartment. It looks much like Seville, with doors to the rest of the apartment and the outside. The hourglass is on a shelf. The skull is an ashtray. A shabby couch, center. A wall of black-bound books.

The door to the outside opens. Don enters in a shabby lounge-lizard outfit and shades, with SANDY, *forty, a corporate exec.*

DON   Well, this is my palace. Not exactly a castle in Spain.

SANDY   No, I wouldn't call it a castle in Spain. Maybe a dump in South Chicago. (*Picks up a pair of panties*)   Yours?

DON   Ah, my dust rag! Thank you. So put your feet up. Or down. Or whatever angle you prefer.

SANDY   What do you pay for this place?

DON   Eighty dollars a month.

SANDY   You're kidding. When did you move in?

DON   Forty-three years ago.

SANDY   Oh. A sense of humor. I like that. (*Don moves in on her. She holds him off.*)   One second, Dick.

DON   It's Don, actually.

SANDY   I ought to tell you, I don't do this every day.

DON   You mean visit a gentleman's flat for light refreshments?

SANDY   No, I mean pick up a stranger for uninhibited fucking.

DON   Well, here I am. The perfect stranger. Let's get uninhibited.

SANDY   Your message light's blinking.

Don hits a button on the phone machine.

WOMAN'S VOICE ON PHONE MACHINE   *This is your date from last night, you vampire! You suck the blood of women and then you throw their lifeless bodies away—*

DON (*Turning it off*)   Wrong number, I guess. Care for a libation, Wendy?

SANDY Excuse me?

DON A drink? A cooling beverage? Is something wrong
. . . Wendy?

SANDY *Sandy.*

DON Sorry. That bar was pretty loud.

SANDY Oh? You mean because my *boyfriend* was shouting?

DON Was that your boyfriend?

SANDY Don't get me started on *him*. Don't get me started on
Todd the rat. Todd the *vermin*.

DON Can I offer you a soothing libation?

SANDY Red wine, no sulfites.

DON Lefty!

Leporello enters in ancient, tattered livery.

LEPORELLO What. What.

DON *Vino rosso per due.*

LEPORELLO *Instamatico,* signore.

DON My butler, Lefty.

SANDY Uh-huh.

LEPORELLO *Charmantissimo.*

DON Would you excuse me, Wendy?

SANDY Sandy.

DON Sandy.—Bad news, Leporello.

LEPORELLO Do tell.

DON I-ay ink-thay I-ay aw-say *er*-hay oo-tay ight-nay.

LEPORELLO Utt-way the *uck*-fay are you talking about?

DON I think I saw Elvira tonight.

LEPORELLO Help me, God, help me, help me!

DON At the bar, disguised as a cocktail waitress.

LEPORELLO But we lost her. In Mexico City, in '49.

DON We lost her in Sydney in '38, Calcutta in '22 . . .

LEPORELLO I'll check the apartment, see if she's busted in.

Leporello hands him drinks, and exits.

DON So, my newfound beauty . . . Is something wrong?

SANDY If I wasn't here, you and your "butler" wouldn't be on the rug fondling each other, now would you?

DON No, no, I let Lefty fondle himself. In private, of course. Do you have the time?

SANDY You have a watch right there on your wrist.

DON I always have this nagging fear that it's stopped on me.

SANDY And a clock up there on the wall.

DON It could be slow.

SANDY Therapy might speed it up. Eight-twenty-two.

DON Excellent.

SANDY Do you have an appointment?

DON No no no no, I'm all yours tonight. And vice versa, I hope.

He goes for her, she fends him off.

SANDY Ground rules. You're not "into" anything, are you? Nipple pins, neck chains, cock locks, butt plugs, golden showers, B and D, S and M, any other acronymic perversion?

DON My only kink is copulation.

SANDY Well I refuse to strap on a dildo.

DON Deal.

SANDY Twice in a lifetime is enough.

There's a knock at the door.

DON Would you excuse me for a second?

He opens the door to MIKE, *twenty-three.*

MIKE Don. Hi. Mike, from 9A—?

DON Yes, Mike. What's up?

MIKE Well I see you got company, I was hoping maybe you could help me out with a personal problem.

DON I am sort of tied up right now . . .

MIKE No, no, no, that's okay, sorry to butt in like this.

DON Maybe another time.

MIKE Absolutely. Anytime. No problem.

DON 'Bye! (*Shuts the door*) So tell me about yourself, ummmm . . .

SANDY Well. My name is still Sandy. Two: I don't sleep around with just anybody. Tonight happens to be a peculiar night.

DON Ah-ha.

SANDY I'm going through something rather painful at the moment.

DON I'm sorry.

SANDY You're not going to ask *why* this is a painful night?

DON It couldn't be your boyfriend . . . ?

SANDY You mean Todd the *rat*? Todd the *VERMIN*? Why should it be painful that my rodent boyfriend rolls over in his sleep, puts his hand on my tit, and says, *"Blow me again, Tiffany"*—?

DON Cheers.

SANDY Why should it be painful that this asshole has also slept, during our time together, with a Kimberley, a Heather, a Joy, and my wizened cleaning lady Imelda?

DON You and Todd have been together a long time?

SANDY Five weeks.

DON Chin-chin.

SANDY You know why I date morons like this? My mother starved me emotionally, so now, if any man says he likes me, I throw myself down and spread my legs.

DON *I* like you.

SANDY Do you really?

DON Very much. Skol.

SANDY Or it could be my father.

DON He starved you?

SANDY No. He died.

DON I'm sorry.

SANDY   I'm sixteen years old, I get knocked up by some nickel-and-dime Don Juan passing through town . . . Hey. You haven't ever been in Illyria, Illinois, have you? Say, twenty-three years ago?

DON   Illyria, Illinois? Um, no, doesn't ring a bell . . .

SANDY   I should hope not.

DON   Lefty?

Leporello enters.

LEPORELLO   Mein Kommandant?

DON   Illyria, Illinois, twenty-three years ago . . . ?

Leporello checks among the shelves of black books.

LEPORELLO   Illyria, Illinois, twenty-three years ago . . .

SANDY   I tell my father I'm pregnant, and *bang,* he drops dead. I give up my little baby to an orphanage . . . I'm sorry. I'm sorry . . .

DON   Look. You're going through a lot. We don't have to do this.

LEPORELLO   *AHEM!*

DON   Actually, yes we do.

SANDY   You're goddamn right we do. I'm gonna get revenge on Todd *and* on the bastard who knocked me up and you are my weapon, Dick.

DON   It's Don, actually.

SANDY   (*Lying down on the couch*)   I hope I'm over this yeast infection . . .

DON   You know, Keats once read me a wonderful—I mean, he once wrote a wonderful poem about love . . .

SANDY   *Hey.* I thought we were having sex.

DON   Yes, let's have sex by all means.

Leporello steps in and whispers to Don.

LEPORELLO   Cool it, Donny. You slept with this one.

DON   I what?

LEPORELLO   She's in the black book. Volume 246. Illyria, Illinois.

DON   Uhhhhhhh Sandy, I'm afraid I must ask you to leave.

SANDY   What do you mean, leave? Penetration was in the air!

DON   The fact is, I have to take a very long trip.

LEPORELLO   Deepest apologies.

DON   Maybe we can meet for coffee sometime.

SANDY   You bastard!

DON   (*Hustling her with Leporello to the door*)   I'm terribly sorry.

SANDY   I don't believe this! (*Knock at door*)   Who's *this*, now? The next girl in line at your Gothic fuck pad?

VOICE   (*O.S.*)   Sandy! Sandy? Are you there?

SANDY   Oh. Beautiful. It's Todd.

DON   Todd?

SANDY   The rat!

TODD   (*O.S.*)   I know you're in there, Sandy! Let me in!

214

DON   You're going to have to leave now.

SANDY   Let him in.

DON   Sandy, you have to leave!

SANDY   I'm glad you finally learned my name. I said let him in! I'll show that bastard I can have a *fling*.

TODD (*O.S.*)   Sandy! Open up!

DON   If I let him in, will you leave?

SANDY   I said LET HIM IN!

Don opens the door and TODD *enters: forty and a suit.*

DON   Hello, Todd.

SANDY   You RAT.

TODD   Sandy, will you come with me?

SANDY   So you found me.

TODD   I followed you here from that disgusting bar.

SANDY   Maybe the same place you met *Tiffany,* and *Heather.*

DON   Can I step in here for a—

TODD   You bastard! Can I tell you something?

DON   I don't have the time.

TODD   My life was totally meaningless until I met Wendy.

DON   Sandy.

TODD   Sandy. My life is still meaningless, but at least I have found somebody who's as fucked up as I am. These have been the five best weeks of my life! Sandy, will you come with me?

SANDY   Sorry, Todd. I just fucked this man into a sexual stupor. Tell him, Dick.

DON   I am in a sexual stupor.

SANDY   How many orgasms have I had?

DON   Does anybody have the time?

SANDY   I bet I had a hundred orgasms tonight. Which is ninety-three more than *you* ever gave me.

DON   Could you two leave, please?

SANDY   How do you feel now, Mr. Fuckover?

TODD   You know what this is, don't you? This is your sister.

SANDY   No, this is not my sister, this is your grandfather.

TODD   Can we not bring my grandfather into this?

SANDY   And what he did with the soup spoon?

TODD   This is the incident with my brother when I was five. Oh GOD, OH GOD! I'M REMEMBERING IT! I'M REMEMBERING IT!

DON   If you two want to stay and have a session, I have to go out.

TODD   Sit down, asshole.

DON   *MOVE IT, TODD!*

TODD   (*Blocking Don's way with his umbrella*)   Make me.

DON *grabs an umbrella from an umbrella stand. Todd thrusts, Don parries, and they're at it. While they swordfight:*

SANDY   Oh sure. Fine. Penis substitutes. That's all men ever know. Well I don't have to stay here and watch this crypto-

216

homoerotic love play. If you want me, you worm, I'll be at home revving up the vibrator, getting more affection from General Electric than *you* ever gave me. (*Suddenly Sandy stops.*)   Wait a minute. WAIT A MINUTE. *FREEZE!* (*Don and Todd freeze.*)   What is that?

DON   It's a skull.

SANDY   And your name is Dick Jackson?

DON   Don Johnson.

SANDY   Todd, that's him.

TODD   That's who.

SANDY   That's him. That's the father of my baby!

DON   I'm the what?

SANDY   *That's the man who killed my father!*

DON   I'm the what?!

SANDY   *That's DON JOHNSON!*

DON   *Dick* Johnson, actually. Jackson.

SANDY   And the bastard looks younger than me! Kill him, Todd.

TODD   What . . . ?

SANDY   Kill him. Take that man's life and I'm yours forever.

TODD   I can't just, you know, kill him.

SANDY   *KILL HIM! KILL HIM! KILL HIM!*

LEPORELLO   Donny, go!

Don runs out and Leporello blocks the door.

SANDY   Get out of my way.

LEPORELLO   Look, don't take this so personally!

SANDY   I said GET OUT OF MY WAY!

Sandy exits, chasing Don.

TODD   *Sandy! We have to talk!*

Todd exits, chasing Sandy. Leporello shuts the door.

LEPORELLO (*To us*)   Four hundred years of this shit, can you imagine? Feels like a thousand, but who's counting. Life kinda flattens out after you pass the big four-oh-oh. And lose all your dough. Yeah, spring of 1896, Mr. Rocket Scientist invests the family fortune in this new invention called the automobile. Great idea, too bad he bought into the *Sam Berkowitz Auto Company*. Straight into the toilet. And Allison the milkmaid? Yeah, well, didn't work out, one thing and another. Sweet Allison the udderly wonderful milkmaid had five kids and nineteen grandchildren. Died in the summer of 1651, peeling potatoes out front of her house. Sixty-eight years old. (*Don comes in through the window.*)   Comes the Don.

DON   Are they gone?

LEPORELLO   You do know how to pick 'em, my prince.

DON (*Collapsing on the couch*)   Oh, God . . .

LEPORELLO   Hey, don't you collapse on me. You gotta go get laid.

DON   Not *again*. Not *again*.

LEPORELLO   *Aufgeht's,* Romeo. *Arriba!*

DON   I still have time.

LEPORELLO   You went out to find *this* cookie at ten this morning.

DON Don't tell me my job. I am the *Don,* remember?

LEPORELLO Do you want to die?

DON Yes I do.

LEPORELLO No you do *not.* And get that shirt off, you look like a dog's dessert.

DON Another day, another Dolores . . . (*He changes his shirt and Leporello spruces him up.*)
Behold my situation, and ponder it.
I get immortality—and squander it,
Serving drinks and wrestling pantyhose.
I have spent my life taking off my clothes. (*He has finished changing.*) Lefty.

LEPORELLO Your Anus?

DON I am completely out of place in this benighted age.

LEPORELLO Actually, you were pretty weird for 1590. Speaking of which, can I get a raise? Since I'm still making two doubloons a year?

DON Celibacy was so sweet . . .

LEPORELLO You're gonna tell *me* about celibacy? I been so busy keeping you in the saddle, I haven't gotten laid since the Crimean War!

DON You're the one who egged me on in the first place. "Get a girlfriend!"

LEPORELLO Pardon me for all those pesky hard-ons you been having.

DON I don't do this because I *like* it, Caliban. Sex is not fun. Sex is my *job.* You don't have to get an erection seven days a week, decade in and decade out.

LEPORELLO What's an erection?

DON Johnny Keats lived twenty-five years and will be remembered for all time. I'll be forgotten the minute I'm gone.

LEPORELLO Hey, none of that "moment-I'm-gone" shit. We *go on*.

DON And now I'm a father . . . ? If that woman was right, I'm a father!

LEPORELLO Listen, Spermbank. The way you been copulating, you coulda populated China.

DON I have a daughter, and I abandoned her . . .

LEPORELLO *Gosh, look, Dad! It's nine-thirty!* (*Knock at door*) It is the fucking Bates Motel around here.

Leporello opens the door.

MIKE Lefty, hi.

LEPORELLO What's up, Mike?

MIKE Well I was wondering if I could talk to Don.

LEPORELLO We're kinda busy right now staying immortal.

MIKE Oh sure. Maybe another time. No problem.

Leporello shuts the door.

LEPORELLO Are you ready, Candide?

DON Wait a minute. What if I run into Elvira?

LEPORELLO Will you get *off* El-Virus? We lost her, okay?

DON What if we didn't? What if she tricks me into having sex?

LEPORELLO Two simple words: *Don't*. And why? Because you *can't*.

DON She doesn't know that.

LEPORELLO Personally I think you hallucinated her.

DON What kind of deal did *she* cut with Lucifer?

LEPORELLO Donny, will you trust me? Elvira will *never, ever*—not in a million eons—it is impossible she could track down us two peons! (*A knock. Leporello opens the door.*) Yes?

Elvira enters, disguised, in a sexy outfit and shades and using a Southern accent.

ELVIRA Kind sir, I apologize for bothering you
And knocking at your door.
I'm looking for apartment 9W.
Would that be on this floor?

(*Don and Leporello exchange a glance.*)

DON & LEPORELLO Nine double-u . . .

DON Would you care to *entrer* . . . ?

ELVIRA Veronica's my moniker and I'm *enchantée.*
But gentlemen, I don't want to intrude.

DON We were just watching some tube.

LEPORELLO An homage to Charles Bronson.

DON How do you do. I'm Don Johnson.
And what luck to meet you, my dear.

ELVIRA (*To audience, lifting her shades*)   Actually,
it's me again. Doña El-*veer*?

LEPORELLO G'night, kids!

Leporello exits.

ELVIRA I hope I didn't scare off your friend.

DON Oh no, he had a few things to attend . . .
To . . . Excuse me, but—
Have I ever seen you somewhere before?

ELVIRA I never saw you in my life
Till I walked through that door.

DON Must be my imagination.

ELVIRA I don't take it amiss.

DON Can I offer you something, Miss Veronica . . . ?

ELVIRA Bliss.

The phone rings and the machine picks up.

SANDY'S VOICE ON PHONE MACHINE *This is Sandy, you prick!*
Don't think you're going to—

DON (*Turning off the machine*) Citibank, *again*?

ELVIRA Now that was kinda strange.

DON City life, huh.

ELVIRA Prob'ly deranged.

Todd looks in the door.

TODD All right, where is she? If you're hiding her, I'll kill you.

DON She's not here, Todd.

TODD I can have you arrested for kidnapping.

DON (*Shutting the door*) Good night, Todd!

ELVIRA   Now that was kinda odd.

DON   Must be the moon.

ELVIRA   This city sure is chock-full o' loons.

Another knock at door.

DON   Go away, Todd!

The door opens to reveal Mike.

MIKE   Actually, it's Mike again. Hello! Sorry! 'Bye!

Mike closes the door.

DON   Shall we utilize the sofa?

ELVIRA   I hope you don't think I'm a loafer
But what if I . . . reclined?

DON   Miss Bliss, how could I possibly mind?

ELVIRA   (*Lying down in a sexy pose*)   But where would *you*
like to set?

DON   Are you *sure* we've never met?

ELVIRA   Girl Scout's honor. Want to bet?

DON   Maybe in Paris? Common Eurail passes?
And what if you take off those glasses?

ELVIRA   Oh no. I couldn't.

DON   You might be more at ease.

ELVIRA   But you see I have this optic disease.
I take these off, things turn to stone.
Something to do with the rods and the cones?

DON   Veronica, would you excuse me for a second?

ELVIRA   For a single solitary tick, I reckon.

DON   And you said your name was—

ELVIRA   Bliss.

DON   (*Takes a black book off the shelf*)   Bliss. Bliss . . .

ELVIRA   You do what you need to, I'll keep on talking.
Furnish some blather. Oh darn it!

DON   A problem?

ELVIRA   A run in my stocking.
Look at that ladder! These nylons were new!

DON   Maybe there's something *I* could do . . . ?

ELVIRA   I know I sound like a martyr,
But this is a particularly sticky garter . . .

DON   I have some digital expertise.

ELVIRA   Oh, would you assist me *puh-lease*? (*They're getting closer, for a kiss.*)
Unless there's someplace else you need to be . . .

DON   Tonight, Miss Bliss, I am totally free.

ELVIRA   Total freedom. What a pleasant curse.

DON   So what can I do?

ELVIRA   Just reach down deep in my velvet purse.

DON   (*Pulling back*)   That's funny.

ELVIRA   A problem?

DON   We're talking in verse. That's odd.

ELVIRA   Maybe it's a sign from God. (*She draws him back.*)
         You know what rhymes with "bliss,"
         Don't you, Don Johnson . . . ?

DON   Where are you from, Veronica?

ELVIRA   Me? I'm from Wisconsin.

DON   And we've never met before today?

ELVIRA   Spent my whole life on a farm, pitchin' hay.
         Playin' the harmonica.

DON   Yet you don't *sound* like Wisconsin.
         More like Kentucky.

ELVIRA   Well my family's from southern Milwaukee.
         The northern flank of the southern tier.

DON JUAN Uh-huh.

ELVIRA   (*Snapping open a fan*)   Is it gettin' kinda warm in
         here?

DON   Goddamn it, Elvira, this is inhuman!

ELVIRA   "Elvira . . ."?

DON   You can drop the act.

ELVIRA   Oh, all right. So how've *you* been?

DON   Get out of here, Elvira.

ELVIRA   Don Juan, you've made my life a sea of tears.

DON   So you've told me for *four hundred years*.

ELVIRA   So I love you! Is that a crime?

DON   We *ended, muchacha*! In 1599!

ELVIRA   Yes, June twenty-eight, the day we began!
                But you won't escape. I have a plan.
                I almost nailed you in Dien Bien Phu.

DON   Ah, right. At the Hotel Déjà Vu.

ELVIRA   Champagne in Kinshasa.
                That was a bubbly time.

DON   Tea beneath a lime tree in Lhasa.

ELVIRA   Sub-lime. Remember the shellfish on the dock?

DON   Elvira, I can't.

ELVIRA   You are so *selfish*!

DON   Do you have a clock?

ELVIRA   Do I repulse you, if I may be rude?

DON   Au contraire,
              You remain the epitome of pulchritude.

ELVIRA   Then what's one more poke to you,
                Who've poked a multitude?

DON   No.

ELVIRA   I know it's a bit sticky.

DON   I have to go.

ELVIRA   Come on, Don Juan. Just a quickie?

DON   (*Starting out*)   No! Never! Goodbye!

ELVIRA   Don Juan, if you sleep with me—I die. (*Don stops at the door.*)
                Just love me once and you'll be rid of me.

DON   It's a lie.

Don Juan in Chicago

ELVIRA	Cold hard fact.
DON	A fabrication to give me pause.
ELVIRA	No, it's in the contract. (*She produces her contract.*) Second clause.
DON	(*Reading the contract*) I have no retort. My brain is weak.
ELVIRA	Well. The ball is in your court.
DON & ELVIRA	So to speak.
ELVIRA	I guess you also cut some deal.
DON	Sí.
ELVIRA	For eternal sex, no doubt. You heel.
DON	I can't send you to eternal torment.
ELVIRA	Hell doesn't terrify me. I've been in hell for centuries. So my beloved enemy, hated friend, Won't you love me and kill me? That's my humble petition. Amen.
DON	I can't.
ELVIRA	Help me, partner. Let me rest.
DON	But there's a good reason.
ELVIRA	Have you no decency? Have you no heart, sir?
DON	No. Listen—
ELVIRA	I don't give a fart, sir. Try your best.
DON	Elvira, please.

ELVIRA   We have a bond, Juan!
          All right, this visit didn't work, alack.
          But don't you work, jerk! *I'll be back!*

Elvira exits, banging the door shut.

Blackout.

End of Act I

ACT II

The same scene, a moment after the door bangs shut behind Elvira.
Don stands exactly where he did. Leporello enters.

LEPORELLO Did her quick, huh. So I guess we're immortal
for another day?

DON It was Elvira.

LEPORELLO Help me, God, help me, help me!

DON She can't die until I make love to her again.

LEPORELLO Wowzer. Okay. I'll pack tonight, we'll call the
movers in the morning and try our luck in Mongolia. Holy
shit, nine-fifteen. You gotta get on your stick. What's the
matter?

DON I could have done the noble thing and I turned her down.

LEPORELLO Well sure you did! I mean *POOF*. What could
you do?

DON I could've slept with her.

LEPORELLO I'm sorry, I couldn't hear you, you had your
head up your ass.

DON Maybe I'll read for a while.

LEPORELLO D. J . . .

DON (*Reading from a book*) ". . . many a time I have been half
in love with easeful death . . ."

LEPORELLO Donny. Donny. Yo! (*To audience*) Can
somebody help me out here? Any of you ladies feel like a
tumble? Here's your big chance. Sleep with the Don, tell all

229

your friends, and you would have my literally undying gratitude. How about you? Donny, I have a gorgeous woman here, first woman right here on the end. See?

DON (*Glancing into audience*) I've slept with her.

LEPORELLO The blonde in row ten.

DON I've slept with her.

LEPORELLO Will you go out and find somebody? Will you copulate, please?

DON I didn't know you were that attached to this world.

LEPORELLO I *love* this world.

DON (*Throwing down his book*) Well, *I don't love this fucking world!*

LEPORELLO Give it a better chance.

DON What, better than four hundred years?

LEPORELLO You always wanted to be a household name! You're in the dictionary!

DON Yes. Don Juan. The biggest dick in history. Famous for fucking.

LEPORELLO People envy you!

DON Pigeons fuck. Pigs fuck. Goldfish fuck. Who envies them?

LEPORELLO *I* do, frankly.

DON Leporello, we've seen twenty generations pass from the earth. Aren't you tired of seeing people die?

LEPORELLO *Hell* no.

DON Sleep with another woman? Why should I?

LEPORELLO Why? I'll tell you why. Because *you owe me,* pal. I have never once said this in four hundred years, but you got an obligation. You don't like the bargain you made? Too bad. You want to go to hell? Fine. But you got no fucking right to take me along with you. You had no fucking right in the first place. So either you leverage me outa this deal, or you find somebody to sleep with. I'm sorry to put this so bluntly.

DON No. No. You have every right. *I'm* sorry.

LEPORELLO And what about this kid? Your daughter? (*A knock at the door*) *Live,* Don. You'll get to meet her!

DON That child is lost.

LEPORELLO She has to be someplace. We'll find her! (*Another knock at the door*) We'll hunt up Wendy-Sandy-Wendy; you can have a family reunion.

DON What could I say to my daughter if she came knocking at that door?

Knock at the door.

LEPORELLO You say, Clean up your room, like all fathers! Don, this is your whole family!

He opens the door to Mike and ZOEY, twenty-three.

ZOEY Hello.

LEPORELLO Well, isn't this delightful. Behold: a fair young maiden on our stoop!

MIKE Hi, Don.

DON "Who are these coming to the sacrifice?
To what green altar, O mysterious priest,
Lead'st thou that heifer lowing at the skies . . ."

ZOEY "Fair youth, beneath the trees, thou canst not leave
Thy song, nor ever can those trees be bare."

DON "For ever wilt thou love—"

ZOEY "—and she be fair."
John Keats. Hello.

MIKE Lefty, this is my girlfriend, Zoey.

LEPORELLO Donny, this is Mike's girlfriend, Zoey.

ZOEY I'm really sorry, us just coming in like this.

DON No, please. Come in further. Don Johnson. How do
you do. (*Kisses her hand*) And you know Keats.

ZOEY Oh, I don't really know about Keats. I don't really
know anything about anything. It's just I learned that poem
in high school and those words are so beautiful.

DON Johnny wrote some wonderful things.

ZOEY He's dead now, you know.

LEPORELLO Donny *is* four hundred years old, heh heh heh.
But come on, kids, sit down! We were just partying here!
And look, Don, they brought us a present!

He starts to take a gift-wrapped box from Zoey.

ZOEY Actually that's a gift for Mike. It's a tie.

LEPORELLO (*Aside to Don*) Is she something, Dondi?

DON Suddenly I have a strange soup of emotions boiling
around my heart.

LEPORELLO So *consummate*! *Consummate*!

DON With not a trace of the sexual.

LEPORELLO   I love it when you're ironic like that. You move in; I'll distract the lunk.—Well, my convenient amigos. What brings you to our humble commode?

ZOEY   Actually, we came over to ask if we should sleep together.

DON & LEPORELLO   Excuse me?

MIKE   Zoey, you shouldn'ta put it like that.

ZOEY   That *is* our question, isn't it? Mr. Johnson—should Mike and me sleep together?

LEPORELLO   Or you and God-knows-who-else, right?

DON   Why are you asking *me*?

ZOEY   Well, every time we see you you're either walking in with a woman, or letting some woman out. Mike said you're running a house of prostitution. Am I right, Mike?

MIKE   You're right, Zo.

ZOEY   *I* said you're just a real Don Juan.

The door opens and Sandy appears.

SANDY   That man is a vulture! He feeds on the bodies of those he—

Leporello closes the door.

LEPORELLO   Political candidate.

MIKE   Anyway, Zoey and me've been going out since seven years tomorrow.

ZOEY   And we pledged eternal love on like our second date.

MIKE   But we've never slept together.

ZOEY We've never slept with anybody.

MIKE Except ourselves.

ZOEY Separately, I mean. I have my place, and Mike has his place . . .

LEPORELLO You don't mind my asking. *Seven years* and this never came up?

MIKE I dunno. It never seemed important, somehow.

ZOEY And there's so much really important stuff to do. We take walks, and we talk. About—you know—the meaning of life. (*Holding up the skull*) What an interesting ashtray.

MIKE Very interesting.

ZOEY Anyway, these days everybody's slept with somebody besides themselves. And I said, there's that man down the hall Don Johnson. Am I right, Mike?

MIKE You're right, Zo.

ZOEY So what do you think? Sex? Or no sex?

LEPORELLO Y'know, Mike, I got a very rare astrolabe in the other room.

MIKE Oh wow, an astrolabe? What's that?

LEPORELLO (*Leading Mike out*) We'll leave you two alone.

Leporello exits with Mike.

ZOEY I've never met a butler before.

DON He's not entirely typical.

ZOEY "He's not entirely typical." God, where does one learn to talk like that?

DON In hell.

ZOEY You know, it's funny. I don't even know you and I trust you. Almost like a father or something.

Mike looks in from Leporello's room.

MIKE How are you doing, Zo?

ZOEY Fine. We're talking about how I trust Don like a father.

MIKE Oh. Okay . . .

Mike goes back out.

ZOEY So Mr. Johnson, will Mike and me go bad if we sleep together?

DON It's just biology, isn't it?

ZOEY Is it?

DON And one only has so much time.

ZOEY Does one?

DON Well, Venice is sinking and the polar caps are melting.

ZOEY But will Mike and me still be *happy*? That's what I want to know.

DON You'll be much happier.

ZOEY You've slept with lots of people. Are *you* happy?

DON Terribly happy. Blissful.

ZOEY You don't look very happy. In fact you look terribly sad. Speaking of hell, it's just like this opera called *Don Giovanni*. Have you ever heard of this opera called *Don Giovanni*, by Moss Hart? Don Juan sleeps with all these women but hell opens up and he falls into the fiery pit.

DON It is only a fable.

ZOEY No, no, no, it's real. Because Don Juan doesn't sleep
with those women with love in his heart. If you live
without love, you've given up your soul. Am I right, Don?

DON You're right, Zoey.

ZOEY My mother slept with somebody for one night and had
me. It's like God said to her, You did this for pleasure, but
now I'll show you the important part. Which is love.

DON So you're an orphan . . .

ZOEY But I do hope to meet my parents in this lifetime.
Mike and me were going out to the Commendatore Diner
for some supper. Would you like to come along, Don?

DON I'd love to.

Leporello enters.

LEPORELLO So how is it going in here?

DON Zoey just invited me to dinner.

LEPORELLO Indeed, indeed?

MIKE Zoey, I thought we were gonna go out by ourselves.

ZOEY But Don is helping us out. Isn't that right, Mike?

MIKE Yeah, but . . .

ZOEY I guess I'd better go change.

MIKE I thought you were going like that.

ZOEY But we have a guest with us, Mike . . .

Zoey and Mike exit.

LEPORELLO How'd you do, Tristan?

DON I didn't do anything.

LEPORELLO I know. You're gonna do it in the cloak room at the restaurant. I *love* that!

DON I'm not going to do anything.

LEPORELLO Wait wait wait wait wait.

DON That is not just a girl.

LEPORELLO It's a girl! Sleep with her!

DON And corrupt her?

LEPORELLO You can't corrupt anybody anymore! Everybody's corrupt now!

DON She's not. She's radiant.

LEPORELLO Did you ever hear the joke about screwing in a lightbulb? How many dons does it take?

Todd appears at the door.

TODD I am going to murder you, Johnson.

DON You can't murder me. Good-bye, Todd!

Todd goes away.

LEPORELLO Please, Don. I got everything to live for.

DON Like what?

LEPORELLO Like my youth! I'm still young! No, I'm not. Okay. Like my wonderful job! What'm I talking about, I'm a fucking slave. Like my living conditions! Like . . . ! Like . . . ! Okay, so I have no reason to live. Does that mean I have no reason to live? Gimme the chance to see the bluebells again. Gimme the chance to find out what a bluebell *is*.

DON   I will not sleep with her.

LEPORELLO   Then you better get a date with somebody else, and pronto!

Thunder and lightning as Mephistopheles appears.

MEPHISTOPHELES   You have a date with *me,* Don Juan!
Sleep with this girl
Or I'll spit you in the hottest hole in Hades,
And you'll roast right where you like it,
Down among the ladies.
You'll blaze away like truth's own torch.
Obey the contract—or scorch!

DON   I'll see you, Satan, at midnight's bell.

MEPHISTOPHELES   Yes, when I come to carry you to hell!

DON   Excuse me. I've got a dinner to go to.

Don exits.

MEPHISTOPHELES   (*To Leporello*)   Boo! (*Leporello faints to the floor.*)
Forgive me, mortals! The devil made me do it!
I had no choice! I-I-I-I—oh, screw it.
Must I, the Very Nearly All-Powerful,
Explain my acts to every begging little get?
The Don was reneging,
I was calling in the debt.
But hark—a visitor. (*Sandy comes in the
window with a knife.*)
Sandy with a stiletto. Heaven forfend.
This is interesting. Attend.

Mephistopheles disappears.

SANDY   Get up. Get up, I said! You pimp.

LEPORELLO Oh. Sandy . . .

SANDY Thank you for remembering my name.

LEPORELLO Y'know, Don would love to talk to you.

SANDY Yes and I'd like to talk to *him*.

LEPORELLO He just went out.

SANDY Good. Your lifeless body will be here to greet him.

LEPORELLO Actually, my lifeless body still has a couple hours yet.

SANDY Die! Die! Die! Die! Die!

She stabs him repeatedly, to no effect.

LEPORELLO Sandy.

SANDY Die, die, die, die, die . . . (*Still no effect*) You're not dead.

LEPORELLO Uh, no.

SANDY Why, why, why, why? This is a Toledo blade!

LEPORELLO Ironically, so am I. But as they say at Ohio State: Toledo, too late.

SANDY Story of my life. Even before I've started I'm beat.

LEPORELLO Want to join me?

SANDY What is that?

LEPORELLO Bourbon on the rocks.

SANDY Make it neat. You know why I do this?

LEPORELLO Lemme guess. A traumatic afternoon with your cousin Bea?

SANDY No, it's me. Me, me, me, me, me! I'm cursed!

LEPORELLO I'll tell you what's weird. We're talking in verse. (*Holding out her drink*) Well cheers, Sandra. Or is it Alexandra?

SANDY Actually, it's Allison.

LEPORELLO Allison . . .? Did you say Allison . . .?!

SANDY You can't stand the name?
It makes your hair stand on end?

LEPORELLO *Au contraire!*
Something else is starting to bend!
Allison, could I ask something strange,
Put the horse behind the cart?
Would you take your fingers
And feel my heart? Is it . . . ?

SANDY It's beating *fast*. Oh boy!

LEPORELLO Beating? It's Beethoven!
It's the fuckin' "Ode to Joy!"

SANDY Wow. The fibrillation is intense!

LEPORELLO So's the genital stimulation.
No offense.
What are you, the Queen of Araby?

SANDY What're *you*? The answer to my therapy?
And invulnerable, too . . . ? What stamina.
Oh, my animus.

LEPORELLO My anima!
Y'know, Channel 37 is screening film noir.

SANDY We could watch it on the couch,
Or in your boudoir.

LEPORELLO   My sheets are pretty scary.
Would you tell me to shove it?

SANDY   On the contrary. I *love* it.

Sandy and Leporello exit to bedroom as Don enters with Zoey and Mike.

ZOEY   How do you know all this stuff? It's like you've been everywhere and done everything.

DON   Well I *am* four hundred years old.

ZOEY   You know I halfway believe it?

DON   Some champagne? What do you say, Mike?

Mike shrugs.

ZOEY   Some days I wish I could make a deal with the devil. No, really. See, I've really had a pretty happy life, only I don't know anything about anything. You seem pretty miserable but you sure do know about stuff. I'd give up some of this happiness for some stuff.

DON   Don't give up an ounce of it. I'll get the champagne.

Don exits.

MIKE   So, Zoey, you want to come back to my place and talk for a while?

ZOEY   I never did give you your anniversary present. Happy anniversary. (*Mike takes the box from her.*)   Go ahead. Open it. I mean, you know it's a tie.

MIKE   Who are you?

ZOEY   What . . . ?

MIKE   Who are you? Who am I talking to, here? Were you always like this and I never noticed, or is this new, tonight?

A guy recites poetry and kisses your hand and suddenly you're a different person? Which person are you, the person who didn't hear me talking at the dinner table? Or are you the person who swore eternal love with me seven years ago tomorrow? I guess I'm not enough for you now, you have to make a deal with the devil to be happy, is that it? You want something more exciting in your life than just being happy. So hang out with somebody else, somebody like Don.

ZOEY   Don't say these things, Mike.

MIKE   You don't want to sleep with me, sleep with him instead.

ZOEY   I don't want to sleep with him. I never even thought of that.

MIKE   What does this say, right here? (*Reads off the paper tag on her gift*) "With love from Zoey." Love. Zoey. How did this word "love" get here? Were you lying when you wrote this word?

ZOEY   No.

MIKE   Eternal love, remember?

ZOEY   I do love you. But . . . maybe we're not so eternal after all.

MIKE   Two strangers can learn how to love each other. How can two people who love each other turn into strangers?

ZOEY   I don't know, Mike. I don't know what's going on with me tonight. I feel so sorry. I don't even know why.

MIKE   Well. Happy anniversary. Happy everything. 'Bye, Zo.

Mike crumples up the paper tag and exits. Don enters with champagne bottle.

DON Where are you going, Mike . . . ? Where's Mike gone to?

ZOEY You better stay away from me. I think you're the devil.

DON Zoey, what is it? What are you talking about.

ZOEY How can this happen? What have you done to me?

DON Zoey, I swear.

ZOEY I think I just broke Mike's heart. This morning I had everything. I was so happy. Somehow I gave it all away . . .

Leporello enters.

LEPORELLO Donny. Listen. Remember I didn't have a reason to live? Oh boy do I have a reason to live, and she's right in that bedroom.

DON I can't talk right now.

LEPORELLO So did you get lucky?

DON I'm sorry, Leporello. We're dying tonight.

LEPORELLO No we are *not* dying tonight. You gotta do that thing and do it fast, and right now you only got one prospect. She's standing right there. You only got an hour till the clock says bong, and don't forget: You are the *Dong*.

Todd enters.

TODD Dick Jackson?

DON Don Johnson.

TODD (*Producing a pistol*) Say your prayers.

ZOEY Oh my God . . . !

DON Zoey, stand behind me.

TODD When you get to hell, tell them Todd the Rat sent you. You bastard, you ruined my life! (*He fires the pistol, but Don keeps standing.*) You bastard! You ruined my life! (*He fires again.*) You bastard! You ruined my life! (*He fires again.*) You bastard, you . . . You should be dead . . . ! (*He fires again.*) *YOU SHOULD BE DEAD!*

Todd exits.

DON Zoey . . . ?

ZOEY Don . . . ?

Mike enters.

MIKE Zoey . . .

ZOEY Mike!

LEPORELLO Don . . .

ZOEY Don . . .

MIKE Don . . .

DON Zoey—are you all right?

ZOEY There's no bullet holes! There's no blood or anything!

DON I guess he must've missed.

ZOEY How could he miss? He fired right at you! What *are* you?

DON I'm a monster, Zoey. Yes, a vampire. But Mike isn't. He's flesh and blood, and he loves you. Don't you, Mike?

MIKE Well sure, I mean . . . Yeah, I'm flesh and blood.

Sandy enters.

SANDY What the hell is going on out here?

LEPORELLO Sweetheart, you got any horny acquaintances might want to come over for a quick and stormy relationship?

SANDY Oh *that's* nice. That's very cute.

LEPORELLO No no no no no. Not for me. For him!

Elvira enters, dressed as in Seville in Act 1.

ELVIRA Don Juan de Tenorio,
For the last time I come to your door.
But not for my wonted favor, señor.

DON Ask me once again and it's yours forever.

ELVIRA I've come to say farewell
Before I join the Convent of Our Savior.

DON Elvira, stop! Not one more rhyme!

ELVIRA I'll spend eternity atoning for my crime.

DON Will you listen to me, darling?

ELVIRA I'll amend my soul, I'll . . . (*Stops*)
Did you say "darling"?

DON I did.

ELVIRA This is pretty goddamn startling.

DON Zoey, the answer to your question is *yes.* Yes, you should sleep together if the person in question is the perfect person. And if, as you say, you do it with love in your heart.

ZOEY Did I say that?

DON This is my perfect person. My life and my light.

ELVIRA Don Juan, is this a joke?

DON No.

ELVIRA More of the usual mirrors and smoke?

DON Call it an eleventh-hour confession.

ELVIRA To wit?

DON I love you, Elvira.

ELVIRA Oh *shit*!

DON If you have any doubt,
Here and now in that bedroom I'll allay it.
I love you, Elvira.

ELVIRA It took you long enough to say it!

DON Elvira, we've been farcing
In and out of doors
Because *my* contract's the opposite of *yours*.

ZOEY Well, Mike. Now I know we're not in Illyria anymore.

DON, SANDY, & LEPORELLO (*GASP!*)

SANDY Did you say . . .

DON Illyria?

LEPORELLO Illyria?

SANDY Illyria?

ZOEY Illyria, Illinois, my home. Actually, my foster home.

DON, SANDY, & LEPORELLO (*GASP!*)

ZOEY Did I say something?

SANDY So you're an orphan?

246

ZOEY Yes, but I do hope to meet my parents someday in this lifetime.

SANDY And how old are you?

ZOEY I'm twenty-three.

DON, SANDY, & LEPORELLO (*GASP!*)

SANDY Do you know who your parents were?

ZOEY All I know is, my mother's name was Wendy. Or Sandy.

DON, SANDY, & LEPORELLO (*GASP!*)

ZOEY Did I say something else?

SANDY *I'm* Wendy!

LEPORELLO Sandy.

SANDY Sandy.

ZOEY You mean . . . ?

SANDY My baby!

ZOEY Mama . . . ?

They embrace.

MIKE Wow. What a small world.

LEPORELLO What a small apartment. Move over, will ya?

DON Ladies and gentleman, time is short and there's much to do. I must go away tonight on a very long trip—with this lady. But first and most lovingly, to bed. So, Zoey, if you and your mother might catch up somewhere in private . . .

ZOEY We could go to our place, Mike.

MIKE Did you say *our* place?

ZOEY   Am I right, Mike?

MIKE   Well . . .

LEPORELLO   Mike, don't look a gift horse in the orifice.

MIKE   You're right, Zo.

ZOEY   Good-bye, Mr. Johnson. Thank you for everything.

DON   It was my profoundest pleasure. (*Kisses Zoey's hand, then shakes Mike's*)   Good-bye, Mike. No hard feelings, I hope.

MIKE   God. About what?

LEPORELLO (*Aside to Don*)   Donny, this is your kid. Aren't you going to tell her?

DON   Only to leave her again? No.

ZOEY   Are you coming, Mom?

SANDY   Lefty? Are *you* coming?

LEPORELLO   Yeah. Uh, listen, my beehive.
Could you come back in a while?
Say, twelve-oh-five?
Adios, my transcendental one.

SANDY   Au revoir. My sentimental one.

Sandy exits with Zoey and Mike.

LEPORELLO   So the Sandys of time have finally run out. Had to happen sometime.

DON   Thank you for everything, down the ages.

LEPORELLO   Probably futile to ask for a raise. Well, guess I'll go change into something cool.

Leporello exits.

DON JUAN	Now we must hurry, love, For we only have the briefest while.
ELVIRA	Yes, I well recall your speedy style.
DON JUAN	This time, till death comes, let's linger. Finger to finger, body to body . . .
ELVIRA	Head to head . . .
DON JUAN	Head to head. There's only one place for it, sweet.
ELVIRA	You mean—?
DON JUAN	Bed.
ELVIRA	Bed?
DON JUAN & ELVIRA	Bed.

A thunderclap as Mephistopheles appears.

MEPHISTOPHELES	Not so fast, my pretties. Trick or treat.
DON JUAN	You can't take us. I have ten minutes to go.
MEPHISTOPHELES	Ah. But listen, Don Juan. (*A church clock chimes loudly.*) Seems your clocks *were* a little slow. Midnight.
DON JUAN	Oh, all right. You won. You always knew you would. Checkmate.
MEPHISTOPHELES	But what the heck, mate. You two've been really *good*. Sensational!
ELVIRA	I'm glad we didn't defraud you of your fun.

MEPHISTOPHELES My dear, this was wildly educational.
Your determination in spite of distress.
This gentleman's endless politesse.
A–plus.
A pity after that to punish him thus.

DON JUAN Thank you for the generosity.

MEPHISTOPHELES I am always moved by the same old thing:
The basest curiosity.
That's why I signed you on:
To find what *you'd* find out, Don Juan.
A man who'd sell his soul
Not to sweeten his tooth
But to dig in the mine of eternal truth,
To plumb the very meaning of life!
I've lived an eon and *I* can't unwind it.
I thought that, given time, *you* might find it.

ELVIRA (*Kneeling*)   Good sir.

MEPHISTOPHELES What's this? Kneeling for mercy, madam?
Some pathetic petition?

ELVIRA The opposite. I beg for perdition.
Though I could wander forever without home
I prefer eternal torment with this man
To immortality alone.

MEPHISTOPHELES Sir, why would you have lain with her
Only to perish?

DON JUAN Because I cherish her, of course.

MEPHISTOPHELES Really, Don Juan,
How can I cast you into eternal fire and ice?
You'd spoil the place by being so *nice*.

Don Juan in Chicago

A gentleman in hell? Very dicey, no mistake.
And what you did today?
The icing on the cake.

DON JUAN   Tonight I reached absolute zero.

MEPHISTOPHELES   Sacrificing yourself for love and kin?
Isn't that what folks call "hero"?

DON JUAN   But I committed the gravest of sins.
I threw my life away,
A gift from the Invincible.

MEPHISTOPHELES   Yes, but you threw it on *principle*.
This hardly savors of hellish behavior.
And love—
Which has always been a mystery to me—
I now understand through you . . . viscerally.
Don Juan, for four centuries I have learned
By looking through your eyes.
And for this, tonight you'll be in paradise.

DON JUAN   But what about eternal torment?

ELVIRA   The fiery pit?

MEPHISTOPHELES   Oh, call it a little test.

DON JUAN   A *test*? That's a bit breezy.

MEPHISTOPHELES   You've won *salvation*. D'you think it's *easy*?
(*Tears up contract*)   Behold. I free you.
You're in clover.

DON JUAN   But not me alone . . .

MEPHISTOPHELES   No, my reluctant Casanova.
Peerless Elvira, too, is freed.

DON JUAN   And Leporello? For him too I plead.

MEPHISTOPHELES   Behold. (*Leporello, Sandy, Zoey, Mike and*
                  Todd appear.)
                  Leporello, I decree,
                  Shall live out his natural life
                  With Sandy,
                  His unnaturally well-analyzed wife.
                  As for Zoey, your incandescent daughter,
                  A diamond of the first water,
                  This more than earthly prize
                  Will bring you glittering descendants,
                  Granting immortality in a different guise.
                  Todd, whose Teutonic name means "death,"
                  Shall walk the earth loveless and alone
                  Until his final heartless breath.
                  Arise, my friends.
                  Your time is over and ended your ancient quest.
                  Open, you heavens, your azure tent!
                  That these two may boff into infinity
                  To their heart's content!
                  Oh my darlings, I shall miss you terribly.

ELVIRA   Is it possible?

DON   We're not going to hell, then . . . !?

MEPHISTOPHELES   Heaven, my prince. Heaven!
                  The celestial palace!
                  Prepare to don the aurora borealis!
                  I give you what I traded for prison:
                  The knowledge of God, the beatific vision
                  With front-row seats!
                  And please give my best to Johnny Keats.
                  Angels are standing in ranks right now,

Archangels are trumpeting at the gate!
I say unto you, my friends,
It was well worth the wait.

(*The chorus gets louder. "Accept, Lord, these blessed beings into eternal life, may they live with you in heaven among your angels unto ages and ages! Holy, holy, holy! Lord God of Hosts!"*)

Accipe, Domine, hos beatos in vitam aeternam, tecum vivant in caelo cum tuis angelis per saecula saeculorum! Sanctus, sanctus, sanctus! Dominus Deus Sabaoth!

Mephistopheles' voice is drowned out by a deafening choir as Don Juan and Elvira join hands and are taken into heaven. White wings sprout from Mephistopheles.

END OF PLAY

THE RED ADDRESS

This play is for Bill Craver

The Red Address was produced by Second Stage Theatre (Carole Rothman, artistic director) in New York City in January 1997. It was directed by Pamela Berlin; the set design was by Christine Jones; the costume design was by David C. Woolard; and the lighting design was by Donald Holder. The cast was as follows:

E. G.	Kevin Anderson
DICK	Ned Eisenberg
ANN, WAITRESS, PROSTITUTE	Welker White
DRIVER	Jon DeVries
LADY	Cady McClain
SOLDIER, MAÎTRE D'	Josh Hamilton

The Red Address was originally presented in March 1991 at The Magic Theatre (Harvey Seifter, artistic director) in San Francisco. Kenn Watt directed. The cast was as follows:

E. G.	C. W. Morgan
DICK	Michael Girardin
ANN, WAITRESS, PROSTITUTE	Erin McCulla
DRIVER	Ron Kaell
LADY	Nancy Shelby
SOLDIER, MAÎTRE D'	Ron Knapp

Time: the present

Place: a middle-size city in America

SCENE ONE

Office. A desk, with a large red apple on it. In the office are E. G. and DICK. E. G.: thirty-five; blue suit. Dick: a little younger; beige suit.

E. G. So who the hell is this guy? What is he? What's he made out of?

DICK Well, they say his name is Joe Driver.

E. G. Okay, what else do we know?

DICK That's actually as much as I found out so far.

E. G. You mean the only thing we got on this man is his *name*?

DICK Come on, I'm still looking into him, Eej.

E. G. I thought you were gonna investigate this guy.

DICK Well, there's not a hell of a lot anybody knows about the man. Plus I'm getting a lot of very conflicting information, E. G.—

E. G. He's eating up the fucking territory, Dick! He just snapped up three of our buttons!

DICK The thing is, nobody knows anything about the guy except that he's from Texas. At least, people *think* he's from Texas . . .

E. G. I thought he was from Chicago.

DICK What I hear is Texas, but like I say, nobody knows for sure.

261

The Red Address

E. G.   There's got to be *some*thing on the guy.

DICK   His outfit's got a very tight lid on it. Plus he's new in the county. He's a goddamn black hole.

E. G.   What about this other guy? Four, five years ago.

DICK   In Chicago.

E. G.   Yeah. That guy put some people outa business.

DICK   That guy put a *lotta* people outa business.

E. G.   So is this Joe Driver the same guy, or is he another guy?

DICK   Frankly, I don't know really yet.

E. G.   You're supposed to be clearing the way for me, Dick.

DICK   I'm doing the best I can!

E. G.   Oh, this is the best you can? Then do *better*. And you want to know why? *Mafia*, Dick.

DICK   Come on . . .

E. G.   The man in Chicago was Mafia.

DICK   Who says he was Mafia?

E. G.   Twenty bucks.

DICK   This guy is from fucking *Dallas* or something!

E. G.   Fifty bucks.

DICK   Does Driver sound like a Mafia name to you?

E. G.   I can't go by names, Dick.

DICK   You gotta go by something.

E. G. Well, by the time you find out who this guy is, we could be *dead,* Dick. *By* the Mafia.

DICK Oh just fuck me, will you, E. G.? Fuck me.

E. G. No. Fuck *me,* Dick. *Fuck. Me. (Pause. They adjust their cuffs, ties, and lapels.)* Now what about Marbella.

DICK Marbella is with us.

E. G. Saved. What about Panko?

DICK Panko is with us too.

E. G. The Pank is saved. What about Boyle?

DICK Actually, Boyle is thinking of going over to Driver.

E. G. That shithead.

DICK He says there have been impurities in the product.

E. G. *Impurities?*

DICK "The product is impure." That is a quote.

E. G. That is a fucking lie.

DICK I did what I could, Eej.

E. G. Boyle owes me for ten thousand gallons. *That's* what's impure. Goddamn pantywaist, hamletizing around all the time. You tell Boyle, I supply pasteurized, homogenized milk.

DICK Fine.

E. G. No radiation, no extra chromosomes.

DICK Pure milk.

E. G. Vitamin D. And Boyle goes over to Driver, he is not saved.

DICK He's fucked.

E. G. And there is gonna be blood on the floor.

DICK Okay. I see Boyle, I'll put it to him. I'll give him your exact words.

ANN *enters.*

ANN Mr. Triplett.

E. G. Yeah. Annie.

ANN Sorry.

E. G. No, we were just having a . . . philosophical conversation here.

ANN Here's the printout you wanted.

E. G. Oh yeah. Thanks.

ANN And your correspondence for today.

E. G. Okay, great, I'll sign it later. Thank you.

ANN I'm going to be leaving in a few minutes. The switchboard's all locked up.

E. G. Already? Jesus, six o'clock. Okay, hang on a second, I'll do this now. (*Starts signing the letters*)

DICK Annie, Annie, Annie . . .

ANN Mr. Bellavacqua called.

E. G. Shit. What did you tell him?

ANN I told him you were busy.

E. G. Great. Put him on my list for tomorrow. (*Hands her a letter*) This can go.

ANN   Mr. Panko called; I put him on the list as well.

E. G.   Great. This can go.

DICK   Say, what's your story, Annie?

ANN   I beg your pardon?

DICK   You been working in this office for how long now, I still don't know the first thing about you. So what's your story?

ANN   I don't have a story.

DICK   Come on. Everybody has a story. Mystery lady.

E. G.   Quit bugging her, Dick.

DICK   I'm just saying . . . You're not nobody.

ANN   Yes. I am nobody. I'm a perfect nobody.

DICK   Well around this office you are somebody.

E. G.   This can go.

DICK   Around this office you are essential. Only you could be anything once you walk out that door at night. And what is that thing, exactly?

E. G.   This one goes registered mail. Thank you, Annie.

ANN   Good night, Mr. Triplett.

E. G.   Good night.

ANN   I'll lock up.

E. G.   Thank you!

Ann exits.

DICK   (*Calls after her*)   Don't do anything I wouldn't do!

E. G. Listen, on this Driver thing . . .

DICK E. G., I'm doing the absolute best I can.

E. G. All I want to know is, is this the same guy from before?

DICK From Chicago.

E. G. So I know who I'm facing off with.

DICK I hear what you're saying. We're men. We understand each other, right?

E. G. Now what the hell am I doing here . . . (*E. G. bites into the apple as he studies the printout.*)

DICK But you know this Driver thing is all part of a larger sociological problem, E. G. I mean, have you noticed how hard it is to tell people apart anymore? Used to be there were more signposts. You know—costumes, uniforms, distinctive touches. You could tell who people were.

E. G. (*Numbers from the printout*) Six, twelve, twenty-three . . .

DICK Like even when I was a kid, priests always wore those long black dresses. If you were on the street and you saw a guy in one of those things, you'd say, Bang, a priest. There was a one-to-one correlation.

E. G. Thirty-five, thirty-seven . . .

DICK Pretty soon they gave up the dresses, but at least they kept the black suits with the white collars.

E. G. Eighty-six . . .

DICK Pretty soon the collars were gone, but at least they still wore black. Now they dumped the black suits and they all dress like golf champions. Same thing with nuns. Same thing with hookers.

E. G.   One-oh-one.

DICK   Used to be you could go down any street and you could always spot the hookers. Any city in the world. Why? Because they dressed like hookers. Now they dress like regular women and you can't tell 'em apart. Meanwhile women are dressing more and more like men. Chances are, if you go down a street and you see somebody dressed like a woman, it's probably a guy. If they're dressed like a hooker, it's *definitely* a guy. And whatever happened to hats?

E. G.   (*Looks up from the printout*)   What the fuck are you talking about?

DICK   Hats! You know?

E. G.   Fucking business . . .

DICK   Now what do you say we go toss back a Bloody Mary.

E. G.   I can't tonight. I promised Lady I'd take her out to dinner.

DICK   Belly up to the bar, E. G.! County beer-drinking champ. Hardball king. Master of the revels.

E. G.   Some other time.

DICK   But hey, that secretary of yours gets better-lookin' all the time. You ever jockeyed for a taste test? King of the old fast make?

E. G.   Yeah right.

DICK   Yeah right. Lady would cut your fucking *balls* off if you ever did. And how is your lovely Southern flower?

E. G.   She's fine.

DICK   She still shopping for a living, or did she get a job?

The Red Address

E. G. Listen . . .

DICK She only loves you for your money, you know.

E. G. Listen—

DICK *I* love you for your personality.

E. G. As long as I'm pulling in dough, Lady doesn't have to work.

DICK Fuck, if I'da known that, I'da married you myself. But hey, what's this secretary's story? She got a boyfriend?

E. G. Why don't you ask her, if you're so interested.

DICK Now wait a minute, Eej. I never, *ever* cheat on Theodora.

E. G. So why are you giving me all this grief?

DICK I'm living *vicariously,* do you mind? I see a girl like that, I want to know all about her. I want to know what she thinks about when she's putting on her panties. I want to know what she talks about with other women in public bathrooms. Now how 'bout a quickie.

E. G. I promised Lady I'd take her out.

DICK This always happens, you know. This is the history of the world.

E. G. What.

DICK A good-looking woman like Lady marries an ugly son-of-a-bitch like you, the guy goes nuts. He can't believe his good fortune he gets to sleep with a beautiful woman every night of his life. It turns his head.

E. G. Okay.

DICK You know there is such a thing as emotional addiction.

E. G. Okay, okay.

DICK Your fate is what you make it. You hear what I'm saying?

E. G. Do I fucking need you to lecture me?

DRIVER *has entered, unnoticed by them. Cowboy boots. Cowboy hat. Fifties. Walks with a cane.*

DICK Just hit me, okay? Hit me.

E. G. I'll hit you some other time . . . (*E. G. notices Driver just now.*) Did somebody let you in here?

DRIVER I let myself in. Are you Mr. Triplett?

E. G. I'm sorry, but the office is closed.

DRIVER My name is Driver. Joe Driver.

E. G. Oh. So you're Joe Driver.

DRIVER You've heard of me, then.

E. G. Yeah, I've heard a little about you.

DRIVER I just thought I'd come over and make myself acquainted.

E. G. This is Dick Braverman, my associate.

DRIVER Hello, Dick.

DICK Hello, Joe.

E. G. So what can I do for you?

DRIVER Well, as you probably know, you and I are in the same business, Mr. Triplett.

E. G.   Uh–huh.

DRIVER   Pasteurized homogenized milk. And as you may have heard, I've already had a little success in this vicinity.

E. G.   Yeah. You just stole three of my best accounts.

DRIVER   Stole?

E. G.   That's what I said.

DRIVER   Hell, I'm not a thief. I'm a businessman, E. G. It's my job to make connections.

E. G.   I think I read about some business you did in Chicago.

DRIVER   In Chicago?

E. G.   Yeah. Four or five years ago.

DRIVER   I've certainly been in Chicago.

E. G.   Well this is *not* Chicago you're in now.

DICK   Fucking right it's not.

E. G.   And we don't need your business in this town.

DICK   Fucking right we don't.

E. G.   Not you *or* your business. So why don't you gather your "connections" and take a flying fuck outa here.

DRIVER   Well, well, well. I'm very glad I came to see you, son. Because it looks like you're just the kind of man I'm looking for.

E. G.   Which is what?

DRIVER   Which is a partner. A potential colleague. Y'see, I won't beat around the bush, Mr. Triplett. I'm looking for a partner. No. Let me rephrase that. I would like to be *your* partner. Obviously what I'm talking about is a merger of our two entities.

E. G. I don't need a partner, Joe.

DRIVER Maybe you don't know *what* you need.

E. G. I'm very satisfied with what I have.

DRIVER Bullshit. Ain't a man alive who's satisfied with what he's got. Not unless he's brain-dead.

E. G. You're with the Mob, right?

DICK Hey, Eej, what the hell kind of a quest—

E. G. It's an easy question. Are you with the Mob?

DRIVER Does Driver sound like a Mafia name to you?

E. G. I can't go by names, Joe.

DRIVER You gotta go by something.

E. G. You coulda changed your name a thousand times over.

DRIVER Now if you're asking do I have acquaintances in the underworld, I'm afraid the answer would have to be yes. It's very hard to go far in this world without one foot in that one.

E. G. I am a purveyor of milk, Joe.

DRIVER I know that.

E. G. Milk, and *just* milk.

DRIVER So am I, E. G.! So am I! And that's the problem, you see, because there cannot be two such purveyors in this here city at the same time. So just to lubricate the situation—how do you like the sound of five million dollars?

DICK Jesus . . . !

DRIVER Cold hard cash, for a 50 percent interest. Are you interested in five million dollars?

E. G. What, so you can make me a front for something?

DRIVER So I can be your partner. You could keep your title, draw a salary, run the day-to-day . . .

E. G. I will not be a front, Joe.

DRIVER Okay, fine.

E. G. For any*thing*, or any*body*.

DRIVER You want to be your own man. That's very noble.

E. G. I *am* my own man, and I am an honest man, and I will not let my business be used as a front for illegal purposes.

DRIVER Y'know maybe you're confusing me with somebody else. Are you sure you're talking to *me*?

E. G. Nobody steamrollers me, Joe.

DRIVER Okay.

E. G. Nobody. *No. Body.*

DRIVER Okay, then. Why don't I rephrase this here offer and give you something to chew on, Mr. Triplett. If you do not want, for any reason, to get into bed with me businesswise, then I say unto you now that within a year, maybe within eight months, maybe even in six—your own outfit will be dead. In other words, you can go into business with me, or you can go *out* of business. Now why don't you think on that and give me a call sometime. (*Puts a card into E. G.'s hand*) Nice meeting you boys.

Driver exits.

DICK What the fuck was that?

E. G. I don't know.

DICK What the fuck was *that,* E. G.? Well fuck *him*! Who does this guy think he is, coming in here delivering ultimatums to you? Does that take some kinda balls, or what?

E. G. Who is this guy, anyway . . .

DICK Yeah, and what is it with this Gary Cooper act? I mean, did you hear that accent? That accent is dime-store, man.

E. G. I want you to find out what he is.

DICK Are you gonna run him out of town, E. G.?

E. G. I don't know.

DICK Five million in cash, that's a lot of *some*thing. Could be, maybe you should take the money and run.

E. G. I will not be a front.

DICK So what are you gonna do, are you gonna—

E. G. I don't *know* what I'm gonna do! Okay? Just back off!

DICK Okay. Okay.

E. G. I'm gonna deal with this.

DICK Okay.

E. G. I'm *dealing*.

DICK Okay. Okay. Well listen. I'm going over to Quigley's for a stiff one. You want to come along?

E. G. No, I'll see you tomorrow.

DICK Okay, well, I'll see you bright and early, buddy. (*He starts out, comes back.*) And don't forget. You are the *king*.

Dick exits. E. G. stands, thoughtful a moment, alone.

E. G. Okay. Now this has happened to me. So am I fucked? Or am I *saved*? Am I fucked, or am I saved . . . ?

He starts to loosen his tie. The scene changes around him.

SCENE TWO

Bedroom. A tall mirror and a closed closet door.

E. G. Lady? Lady . . . ?

E. G. takes off his jacket, then stands deep in thought unbuttoning his shirt. LADY comes up behind E. G., carrying shopping bags. Twenties. Soft Southern accent. White dress, white purse, white high heels.

LADY Wake up, daydreamer.

E. G. Hey. There's my Lady.

LADY There's my man. Gimme kiss. (*They kiss.*) Gimme another. (*They kiss again, longer.*)

E. G. How's that?

LADY Sweet as cherry pie. Are you okay, baby? What's the matter?

E. G. No. Fine. Nothing.

LADY Did you not have a good day?

E. G. No. Yeah. It was good. Did *you* have a good day?

LADY Well I hardly sat down since I left here, if you want to call that a good day.

E. G. And what was your itinerary?

LADY First I went to the mall, and then I had some lunch, and then I went to the museum, and then I fed the pigeons in the park, and then I went *back* to the mall . . .

E. G. This outfit is new.

LADY This outfit is new. And do we like it?

E. G. We like it very much. And did we buy anything else on this junket?

LADY Oh, a few things. A few things . . .

E. G. Yeah? Like some nice sexy lingerie?

LADY You mean like a pair of lacy panties . . . ? (*She takes a pair of black panties out of a shopping bag.*)

E. G. Ohh hey. Nice. Let me feel. (*He touches the fabric.*) Very nice. Nice fabric.

LADY That's enough, now. You'll get all excited. (*She tosses them back into the bag.*) And we still got dinner to go to.

E. G. Actually, would you mind if we stayed in tonight, honey?

LADY No, 'course not!

E. G. All I want to do is relax.

LADY Baby, you name it—(*Kisses him*)—you got it.

E. G. Oh yeah? The moon and the stars?

LADY You got 'em. And the earth?

E. G. No, the earth is yours.

LADY All mine?

E. G. The whole wide world. Change now?

LADY Gimme kiss first. (*Kiss*) Now change. (*They begin to change into robes.*) I saw something today.

E. G. Yeah, what did you see?

LADY Three hummingbirds in our own backyard. *Three* hummingbirds. All over that one gardenia plant.

E. G. Sounds pretty beautiful.

LADY Like three little brown blurs over the flowers. Gave me just a little shiver. Do you think it was a sign? A sign of something?

E. G. Coulda been a sign.

LADY But what was it a sign *of* . . . ?

E. G. That is always the question.

LADY Are you positive you're okay? Did you not eat your apple?

E. G. Yeah! Yeah . . .

LADY I have been a little worried about you, baby.

E. G. Little tired, is all.

LADY Did *you* see anything today?

E. G. Oh, yeah. Four walls and a lot of fluorescent lights.

LADY Come on, you must've seen *some*thing.

E. G. Six thousand invoices.

LADY Did you make a million dollars?

E. G. Sure, sure. Five million . . .

LADY I wish *I* had had that kinda day.

E. G. You know what I think, Lady?

LADY What. What do you think?

E. G. I think men are going to be obsolete in a hundred years.

LADY I beg your pardon? Did you say obsolete?

E. G. Yep. And in a coupla thousand years, totally extinct.

LADY Do you have any good reason *why*?

E. G. Nobody's gonna need 'em anymore. Machines'll be able to do all the heavy work. Missiles and laser beams are gonna fight the wars long-distance.

LADY What are women going to be needed for?

E. G. Running the machines. Having kids.

LADY They'll be making kids in test tubes. They are already.

E. G. Okay. So I guess nobody'll need anybody. Who cares. What's the difference.

LADY What's the matter? Are you feeling a little panicky, hon?

E. G. What, about going extinct? Hell no. *I* won't be around for it. Anyway I'm not interested in men. I'm interested in women.

LADY Luckily for me.

E. G. Maybe whoever's running the future will keep a few men around as a tourist attraction. You know—like pandas. You'll be able to visit 'em at the zoo. They'll sit around in a cage, with a sign on it. "American guys. Last four specimens."

LADY   Sure. And they'll do shows for people.

E. G.   You understand my theory.

LADY   Some trainer'll bring 'em out and they'll play cards, and drink beer . . . read porno magazines . . .

E. G.   Watch football.

LADY   And they'll talk like men, so the folks outside the cage can hear what men sounded like back in the good old days.

E. G.   Like how.

LADY   You know. The way men talk. The way you talk at the office. "You want to take that fucking attitude with me? You take that fucking attitude with me. I'll show you some fucking attitude. Did you see that fucking game last night? Was that fucking incredible? Fuck you! Fuck me? Fuck you fuck me."

E. G.   That's a pretty fair imitation of a man.

LADY   Did I leave anything out?

E. G.   Maybe one or two fucks.

LADY   *Fuck. Fuck.*

E. G.   Maybe *everybody*'ll go extinct. Men'll get a little smaller and women'll get a little bigger. Gradually they'll just start to blend into each other.

LADY   And meet somewhere in the middle.

E. G.   Yeah.

LADY   Well I wouldn't mind meeting somewhere in the middle. And blending. And I don't mean in a thousand years.

E. G.   Oh. So you crave my incredible manhood.

LADY No, I crave *you*. C'mere, caveman. (*She pulls him onto the bed.*) I don't know about the future, but *I'll* always be able to use a man.

E. G. Any man?

LADY This man. And I don't want my babies born in test tubes. I want 'em born in me.

E. G. It's a deal.

LADY What'll you have? Boy or girl?

E. G. One of each. No—two of each.

LADY Okay well you just give me the sign. And we will get to work making some beautiful Tripletts.

E. G. Lady.

LADY Yes, love.

E. G. Don't ever change. Don't ever be any different from what you are, this minute. I just mean . . . everything else in the world changes. I want you to stay exactly what you are.

LADY I'll do everything in my power.

E. G. Where did you *come* from, anyway?

LADY You picked me up on a business trip. Remember?

E. G. Yeah, I remember.

LADY And I saw right into you, mister.

E. G. Oh you saw through me, huh.

LADY Like a piece of glass. But will you feel that neck? That is some big Boy Scout knot. Feels like Triplett Associates to me. Is that the business you got tied up in there?

E. G.   That's the business. Ouch!

LADY   Yep. There's Mr. Bellavacqua . . .

E. G.   Mmph.

LADY   And there's Mr. Panko . . .

E. G.   *Mmph.*

LADY   And there's the Businessmen's Basketball Team . . .

E. G.   *Mmph.*

LADY   And there's your good buddy Dick.

E. G.   Dick . . . ! (*He moves away.*)   Yeah, I bet Dick's back there today. Right on the back of my neck.

LADY   Dick wasn't up to his usual stellar performance today?

E. G.   Dick can't seem to tell two people apart these days. "Maybe this person's from Texas, maybe he's from Jupiter."

LADY   Maybe it's a lack of brainpower.

E. G.   You know, it's not too suprising if men go obsolete. Men are antiques already. You know what it means, being a man anymore? It means being an asshole. That's it. An *asshole*.

LADY   You *did* have a hard day, didn't you.

E. G.   Lady, what would you say if I sold the business?

LADY   Sold the business . . . ?

E. G.   Well, not sold it; I mean what if I took a partner.

LADY   There's nothing wrong with a partner, per se . . .

E. G.   It's this guy Joe Driver.

LADY   Oh, him.

E. G.   Yeah. Him. He made me an offer.

LADY   You're not going to take it, are you?

E. G.   Thing is, it's five million dollars.

LADY   We don't want five million dollars. Not from the likes of a Mr. Driver.

E. G.   Lady—Lady, I'm in deep already. I'm up to here in loans. Now we got customers jumping ship.

LADY   So offer your customers a discount.

E. G.   A discount.

LADY   Sure. Five percent, 10 percent. You have to be nicer to your customers.

E. G.   Thing is, you and me could take all this money and . . . I don't know. Run away to the South Seas. Pretty soon Fiji's gonna look like Columbus, Ohio. Might as well go see it before it disappears.

LADY   *I'll* go talk to this Joe Driver.

E. G.   Oh you will, huh.

LADY   Uh-huh. I'll say to him, Mr. Driver, my husband has spent ten years getting this business on its feet and the hell if some . . .

E. G.   Artificial cowboy.

LADY   . . . artificial cowboy is gonna weasel in on it. And we don't do business with people we don't know, Mr. Driver.

E. G.   Sounds good. I'll send you in.

LADY   Or why don't you let *me* take over the business and you take a sabbatical.

E. G.   Oh you want to take over the business.

LADY   Then you could stay home. Or go shop at the mall for me.

E. G.   Uh-uh.

LADY   I bet I could triple your business in a year.

E. G.   Uh-uh. No way.

LADY   E. G., I need *some*thing to do besides shopping all day.

E. G.   You're free, Lady. You enjoy your freedom.

LADY   So what are you going to do about this Mr. Driver?

E. G.   Lady, if the business goes down, we lose everything. We could lose our house.

LADY   But you *are* this business.

E. G.   Yeah, and when did I ever turn into "this business"?

LADY   You couldn't live with yourself if you went in with him.

E. G.   Okay, look. Could we not talk about the business anymore?

LADY   I know you, baby.

E. G.   I'm not *at* the business. I don't see how come I have to sit around, at home, and talk about the fucking business.

LADY   I'm sorry.

E. G.   Fuck. *Fuck!* The *business!* (*Small pause*)   I'm sorry.

LADY   You poor baby. Come here. Come on.

E. G. (*Remains where he is*)   I did see something today, Lady.

LADY   What. What did you see?

E. G.   I saw a dog under a car. I didn't see it first, I heard it— going up the street by the bank, I heard all these people shouting, and I turn around and I see this car—only what the guy inside didn't know was, there was a dog under the car. He had hit a dog and I guess the collar got caught on the chassis—anyway, this guy was dragging it underneath, scraping the skin right off the thing. The dog is barking and screaming; I guess the guy couldn't hear it over the motor. All these people go chasing after him yelling at him to stop. By the time he finally got to the light, the dog was dead.

LADY   This was a wicked day.

E. G.   I swear to God, Lady, this thing is turning me inside out.

LADY   It sounds to me like you need a little relaxation.

E. G.   Goddamn right I do.

LADY   Looks to me like you need a little distraction.

E. G.   Yeah, if I could just . . . *relax,* a little . . .

LADY   Well, I have an idea.

E. G.   Oh yeah, what?

LADY   Do you know what I think you need?

E. G.   What do I need.

LADY   I think you need a visit to the red address. (*She pronounces that with the accent on the last syllable. There is a distinct silence.*)   Does that sound interesting? Would you like to go to the red address?

E. G.   Maybe.

LADY   Maybe . . . ? (*E. G. says nothing.*)   I think it might be kind of fun. (*E. G. says nothing.*)   So are you interested? (*E. G. says nothing.*)   I'll bet you *are* interested. (*E. G. says nothing.*)   I think you're *very* interested. (*E. G. says nothing.*)   Do you want to go to the red address?

E. G.   I could go to the red address.

LADY   All right, then, good. Why don't you start . . . right . . . here. (*She takes out the pair of panties she had shown him before and holds them out.*)

E. G.   But you bought those for you.

LADY   No, I bought *this* pair for you. So go ahead. Be my guest. (*He takes them from her and pulls them on under his robe. When he has them on he stands quite still.*)   Now how do those panties feel?

E. G.   They feel good.

LADY   Do they fit all right?

E. G.   Yeah, they're perfect.

LADY   The lace doesn't rub too much?

E. G.   No. It's good. It's good.

LADY   Good. Now how about a nice pair of stockings. (*She hands him a pair. E. G. sits on the edge of the bed and starts to pull them on.*)   You can take your time, you know. We've got all night. And I seem to remember that that's a kind of nylons you particularly like.

E. G.   I do like this kind.

LADY   Very sheer.

E. G. Yeah. Very silky.

LADY Well if you like the nylon, maybe what you want to try is a pair of real silk.

E. G. Silk stockings . . . ?

LADY Yeah, maybe you want some real silk stockings, for those particularly stressful days. And while you're wearing 'em you can think about all those thousands and thousands of tiny little worms that went to so much trouble making those threads that make you feel so good . . .

E. G. I love this new outfit you got. Where did we find this?

LADY At a tiny little shop called Souvenir.

E. G. What, that place at the mall? Behind the Rainbow Lanes?

LADY Mmm-hmmm.

E. G. I saw a dress in the window there. A blue dress with like a darker thing down the side here.

LADY Was it iridescent satin? Flared at the bottom?

E. G. Yeah, it had a flounce around the edge.

LADY I saw that dress. That was pretty.

E. G. They had this great black dress too. Net sleeves.

LADY Black net sleeves, huh. Now how do those stockings feel?

E. G. They feel good.

LADY Well since you're in the mood . . . (*She takes a box from one of the shopping bags.*) Happy whatever. Merry un-birthday.

E. G. What, for me?

LADY Do you see anybody else in this room?

E. G. (*Opening the box and seeing what's inside*) Oh boy, Lady . . .

LADY Do you like them?

E. G. (*Taking a pair of red high heels out of the box*) Oh *boy!* These are great!

LADY Try them on, see if they fit.

E. G. Lady, these are beautiful.

LADY I kind of thought you might like them.

E. G. Are they Italian?

LADY Uh-huh.

E. G. Nice leather. How much?

LADY You'll see when the bill comes. How do they feel? Do they fit?

E. G. They're perfect. Thank you. (*Kisses her*) Thank you. (*Kisses her*) Thank you.

LADY Walk around a little. Let's see. (*He walks in the shoes and looks in the mirror.*) *Very* becoming.

E. G. I like this heel. These are terrific.

LADY Now I want you to promise me something, baby.

E. G. You name it. You got it.

LADY Promise me you won't sell to Mr. Driver.

E. G. Lady . . .

LADY I want a promise.

E. G. I don't have any answers on that.

LADY   Your answer is so simple, baby. Everything is good. Everything is fine. You're on your way to the red address.

E. G.   Yeah.

LADY   Now do you promise you won't go in with Mr. Driver?

E. G.   I promise.

LADY   So do you want to go to the red address now?

E. G.   Can I go to the red address?

LADY   You know the way.

E. G. opens the closet door and reveals a red dress hanging there.

E. G.   Will you help me into it?

LADY   (*As she zips him into it*)   Maybe one of these days I'm gonna tiptoe back to that shop called Souvenir and buy somebody a little treat. So he can have a white address, and a blue address, and a black address . . . All the colors of the rainbow. Now let's see. (*E. G. stands for her to see.*)   Turn. (*He turns.*)   Walk a little bit. Yes, that dress really becomes you.

E. G.   God I love this dress.

LADY   It is a very nice address.

E. G.   I love that sound it makes when I move. That whisper.

LADY   It's beautiful.

E. G.   Do you hear that whisper?

LADY   It's beautiful. You are so beautiful.

E. G. stands looking into the mirror. The scene changes.

SCENE THREE

Restaurant. Dick at a table with Driver.

DICK Joe, do you know that you're a hell of an elusive guy to get ahold of?

DRIVER Is that so?

DICK Elusive is not the word.

DRIVER Hell, I'm not elusive. I'm right here, Dick!

DICK We practically had to hire a private detective to find you. We send letters, we make phone calls—nobody knows where you are.

DRIVER People knew where I was.

DICK Your secretary didn't know where you were.

DRIVER My secretary knew exactly where I was.

DICK She practically said she never heard of you. Joe Driver? Never heard of him!

DRIVER Maybe she was just a little confused about who *you* were, Dick. (*He shuffles a deck of cards on the table.*)   As it is, I couldn't have talked to you boys anyway, since I got called away on some unexpected business.

DICK Anything you can talk about freely?

DRIVER I can say that this business included some time on a boat. Two days on a boat with a woman and a pair of trained dogs. And when I say a woman, Dick, I mean a very, very beautiful woman.

DICK I hear you. What do you mean when you say dogs?

DRIVER I'm talking Dobermans.

DICK Was this a longtime romance between you and these dogs? Or just a passing flirtation?—Just kidding, Joe, just . . .

DRIVER Is your boss gonna be here on time, or what?

DICK Always. E. G. sets up a meeting, he is there promptly on time, so you don't have to worry about him.

WAITRESS *enters with a bottle of wine.*

WAITRESS A bottle of Chateau Rouge.

DICK There she is. There's the girl of my dreams.

WAITRESS Would one of you like to taste it?

DICK That's okay, honey, how 'bout if we trust you. Thank you. (*Waitress leaves the bottle and exits.*) So anyway, E. G. and me were talking, and—the what? The waitress?

DRIVER That is some delicious-looking gal.

DICK Mmm-*hmm.*

DRIVER I wouldn't mind putting a little salt on that tail.

DICK No sirree. Only what about your friend?

DRIVER My friend?

DICK You know—the woman, the boat. The dogs.

DRIVER That woman is history, Dick.

DICK You mean personal history or medical history? Just kidding, Joe, just . . .

DRIVER You know, Dick, I am not looking at that girl out of interest. I am looking at her out of *necessity.* Because you see, if I don't have a woman every day, I get these terrible blinding headaches.

DICK   I can sympathize.

DRIVER   What you might call the spermatic migraine.

DICK   My wife has the opposite problem.

DRIVER   Are you familiar with the principles of acupuncture, Dick?

DICK   Acupuncture. You mean the Chinese needles?

DRIVER   The basic idea behind acupuncture is that the human body is an organic whole. And if you know which part of this whole affects which other part, you can take away pain by putting a pin in the right pressure point. For example, if you have a backache, you might have to put a needle into the sole of your foot. If you have a pain in your heart, you might have to put a needle into your arm.

DICK   And if you have a pain in your head, you might have to put your pin into somebody else.

DRIVER   Exactly, Dick. Exactly. And when the pain is on me, I don't care *what* I fuck. Just so long as I put that needle in.

DICK   Uh-huh. Uh-huh . . .

DRIVER   What's the matter, Dick? Are you afraid I might try to fuck you?

DICK   No! Hell no. And hey, nobody fucks me anyway. I'm not fuckable.

DRIVER   Is that so. And here I thought for the right amount of money I could have you bending right over this here table.

DICK   Yeah, well. There ain't enough money in the world for that kinda activity.

DRIVER   Mm-hmm. Just what are you making where you are now, Dick?

DICK   Whoa, whoa, whoa. Hey. That is classified information.

DRIVER   I'm just saying, I'm always looking for a few good men. Individuals who want to rise in the world. Seize an opportunity.

DICK   Listen. That's very generous, but—

DRIVER   So where the hell is your goddamn boss?

E. G. enters, carrying his briefcase.

DICK   There he is. There's the man. And right on time.

DRIVER (*Shaking hands*)   E. G., good to see you.

E. G.   How are you, Joe.

DRIVER   I'm superior, thank you.

E. G.   You two talking business?

DICK   Business? Hell no.

DRIVER   Just jawing away here.

DICK   Yeah, Joe was just briefing me on the principles of acupuncture.

E. G.   Acupuncture . . .

DRIVER   Yes sir—pressure points and painkillers. Right there you got all of human civilization in a nutshell.

E. G.   I'll have to take your word.

DRIVER   Well sit down, sit down. Have a glass of red and let's deal.

E. G. (*Remains standing*)   There's gonna be no deal, Joe.

DRIVER Oh. Uh-huh.

E. G. No merger. No deal. Nothing.

DICK E. G . . .

E. G. Yeah. *Nothing.*

DRIVER What do you think of that, Mr. Braverman?

E. G. I will not be a dog under a car, Joe.

DRIVER A dog under a car. Is that some kinda local reference? Translate for me.

E. G. *Fuck you.*

DRIVER Oh. Uh-huh.

DICK Hey, Eej . . .

E. G. You hear me, Joe?

DRIVER I am listening.

E. G. *Fuck. You.*

DRIVER You're repeating yourself now, son.

E. G. Look, I don't know who the fuck you are, or where the fuck you come from, I don't give a fuck who you represent, I have spent ten years getting my business on its feet and the hell if some artificial cowboy is gonna come weasel in on it. I don't know why you picked me for this, maybe I did something to you in another lifetime, maybe you thought I was gonna roll right over, but why don't you go find some other sucker to play your asshole game. You know why? 'Cause I'm an impostor. Yeah. I'm not a businessman. I'm a *working* man. I do my work, I do my work honestly, I do not work with people I don't know, and I do not *like* you. So fuck you, and I got nothing more to say.

DRIVER Just a second, just a second. *I* got something to say.

DICK You know, E. G., maybe there is a middle ground here someplace.

E. G. What, I'm supposed to negotiate with *this*?

DRIVER You say you don't work with people you don't know? But who do you know, Mr. Triplett? Who do you really know?

E. G. I sure as hell don't know you.

DRIVER Do you think you know this man? I bet you'd say this man was your friend, correct? But how do you know what he does when he's out of the sight of you, or in the privacy of his own home? Maybe this man is a child molester. Maybe he's a morphine addict. Maybe he's impotent.

DICK Now hey, come on now.

E. G. You can know a few things about a person.

DRIVER Maybe when he goes home he likes to put on a dress. Yeah. Maybe he likes to prance around in a set of high heels. You know there are people like that in this world.

DICK Not in *this* town.

DRIVER Yep. There are married men who go home and dress up as ladies in private. *Real* impostors.

DICK Not in this town.

DRIVER Why, there are respectable people who do all kinds of things could ruin their good name just like that—if those things got around the community.

DICK Except there is no dirt on E. G. Triplett.

DRIVER But if you got nothing more to say, E. G.—then what's to say? (*E. G. says nothing.*) I see you're still standing there.

DICK Come on, Eej, take a seat, let's have a real conversation.

DRIVER You got something to say to me now, besides "fuck you"? Or have you been overcome by a sudden strange ambivalence?

E. G. Why me?

DRIVER What's that, son?

E. G. Why did you pick me for this? And what's all these games, why didn't you just run me out of business?

DRIVER Hell, that ain't very sporting. Not much fun in that. And you don't understand. I'm here to *help* you, son, take you under my wing.

E. G. Yeah, right. To turn my business into a shell.

DRIVER Pshaw. Your business is a shell already. It's an empty facade. One breath, I could blow it right over.

DICK Now hey, hey . . .

E. G. So why is this "shell" worth five million dollars to you?

DRIVER You know, the value of things is a funny thing. But I tell you what, E. G.—five million dollars don't seem right? Okay. Let's make it ten.

DICK Jesus.

DRIVER Or—you name your own price.

DICK *Jesus,* Eej.

DRIVER   Come on. Let's dicker. Just what is this business worth to you?

E. G.   You'd pay ten million dollars for a facade.

DRIVER   For 50 percent of it.

E. G.   Why? When you could just take it.

DRIVER   Maybe because I like you.

E. G.   My business isn't worth ten million. It isn't worth five.

DRIVER   It is to me.

E. G.   It isn't worth one.

DICK   Well hey, it's worth *one* . . .

DRIVER   Your *name* is worth ten million. In this town, you have a *very* good name. No dirt on E. G. Triplett, as your friend says. And I would love to have a piece of that name. So would you like ten million dollars, Mr. Triplett? Or what would you like? Do you know what you would like? Why don't you tell us what you'd like?

DICK   Ten million bucks, E. G . . . !

DRIVER   Are you a gambling man, Mr. Triplett? Do you like to take a chance?

E. G.   Sometimes.

DRIVER   Are you familiar with the ancient Oriental system called the I Ching?

E. G.   No. Never heard of it.

DRIVER   Fascinating little game. Uses random chance to help you make decisions.

E. G.   The hell does this have to do with me?

DRIVER Everything. Now you see, the Ching says that everything in the world at every moment is telling you something. Maybe the world is telling you, "Be calm" right now. Maybe it's saying, "Be aggressive." Maybe it's saying, "Do this deal."

E. G. And what.

DRIVER Well you take these cards, for example. Just an ordinary deck of cards. Let's say we draw cards, and the deal is, you get the higher card you go in as my partner, you draw the lower card you're back where you are now. If it's your fate to go in with me, you could not miss drawing a high card. If it's your fate to go this alone, you must draw the lower card. Do you understand, E. G.? Everything that happens, *has* to happen.

E. G. And so what?

DRIVER There's the cards. Care to draw?

E. G. What, you mean . . . Play this game? For real?

DRIVER For ten million dollars.

DICK Jesus H. Christ.

DRIVER *If* you draw the high card. Draw the low card— nothing's changed. We fight this out man to man.

E. G. What if I don't want to play?

DRIVER Oh, I think it's in your interest to play. A man who wants to preserve a good name like yours.

DICK Hey, we're not talking names here, we're talking business.

DRIVER Indeed. Indeed. But into every life a little dirt may fall.

E. G. How do I know that deck isn't stacked?

DRIVER Shuffle it yourself. Crack open a fresh one, if you think it'll make a difference. Are you man enough to trust in fate, if you won't trust me?

DICK You know you got nothing to lose, E. G.

DRIVER Well said, sir. What do you have to lose?

E. G. What have I got to lose?

DICK Ten million bucks.

DRIVER Well you can't hamletize around forever like some goddamn pantywaist. Do I take my cards and go home?

E. G. (*Sitting down*) No. Yeah. Okay. Come on. Let's play.

DRIVER Good. Good. So pick a card, any card. Be as random as you can possibly be. Just remember, E. G.: Everything that happens, has to happen. Now draw.

E. G. Okay.

E. G. reaches again but is interrupted as the waitress enters.

WAITRESS Excuse me. Is one of you a Mr. Triplett?

E. G. That's me.

WAITRESS There's a call for you. They said it's important.

DRIVER You see that, E. G.? Maybe fate doesn't want you to draw just yet.

E. G. I'll be right back.

E. G. exits.

DRIVER Don't you love suspense, Dick?

DICK *Oh,* yeah. *Oh,* yeah.

DRIVER Sure tells you you're still alive, doesn't it. Is E. G. gonna draw the right card or the wrong card? And what is the right card?

DICK Anything can happen.

DRIVER E. G.'s outfit goes down, that would be a tragedy.

DICK Listen, E. G.'s operation is *still* the best in town. And it's an honor to work for the guy.

DRIVER E. G. is a good man.

DICK E. G. is a *very* good man. And a good *businessman*. The guy's got three balls between his legs.

DRIVER All I'm saying is, my offer of employment remains open.

DICK Listen. I do have loyalties you know.

DRIVER Maybe you want to go home and sleep on this, talk it over with the wife. Be loyal to *her*.

E. G. enters.

DICK So what's up, E. G.? Some kind of news? What's the matter?

E. G. Lady is dead.

The scene changes.

SCENE FOUR

Jail. The strong spot of an interrogation light on a YOUNG SOLDIER.

SOLDIER Yes, sir. I was part of it. But I was not alone. And you gotta understand the circumstances. It's, like, the three of us—I mean Corporal McMann and Spec 4 Johnson and

me—we had an overnight pass, only there is not a heck of a
lot to do in this town. Frankie had borrowed, I mean
Corporal McMann had borrowed a car from some girl he
knew, only this individual had to like visit her grandmother
or something—no action there, right? So the three of us
decide we're gonna spend the day bowling together at that
place by the mall. You know, the Rainbow Lanes? Figured
we could get a little mellow, show off the uniforms, finesse
a coupla girls. You people got uniforms, you know how
that works.

Am I talking too fast? Sir? Are you getting all this?

Anyway we're over at the diner there having some
breakfast and waiting for this guy Inky to show up. Inky is
this lone star supposed to have access to substances—reds
and blues, magic powders, various pills, and the like. Only
we're waiting and waiting, breakfast is over, we're out there
by the car now drinking beer and getting rather ticked off
'cause there's still no friggin' Inky and I also need some
serious relaxation. The point being, once we get high, how
can we obtain some female companionship? Frankie knows
this ninth grader at the school who'll trade sexual favors for
money but we gotta wait until recess to see her—can you
dig that?—meanwhile there's still no Inky, we decide frig it,
we'll hit the Rainbow Lanes and take potluck, when outa
nowhere . . . this woman goes walking by. A real Southern
flower, wearing this nice sweet summer dress.

Lady crosses the stage in a pool of light. She exits. Her light fades.

This is the victim I'm talking about now.

Most of the stores are just opening up, so there aren't too
many cars in the lot, a few people are going in and out, I'm
feeling the effects of the beer, I say hello to the woman in a
very nice way. She says nothing back. She just walks on by.
Frankie says something like, Stuck-up bitch—that's his

style—Johnson, his eyes are poppin' outa his head; *I* say to
her, Hi, again. Louder. What's the matter, honey, I say, you
don't like soldiers? Just trying to engage her in friendly
conversation. But the fox is looking for her keys now, coupla
spaces away, making like she's "ignoring" us, right? Frankie
gives me the nudge, I walk over and I say hi again, only this
time I plant this big, wet kiss on her. Just for a goof. I got my
tongue like all over her face. The problem is she pushes me
away and this was her mistake because I bang my elbow up
against her car, and for some reason this got me like really,
really angry. She's trying to get into her car now—I pull her
out. She says, I'll scream. I say, Oh yeah?, and *bam,* I slug her,
and her lights go out, what am I supposed to do now? I got
this unconscious body on my hands. So, I pack her into the
backseat of the car, the one we're utilizing. Well Frankie, he's
all hot to trot, he says we should take advantage of this
opportunity, he offers to sit on her face while I engage in
sexual relations with her, which I admit I did so. Only the
thing is, this is all happening in broad daylight in this parking
lot, right? All these people are driving by—is anybody paying
any attention? Is anybody trying to stop me? Uh-uh. So I
finish and Frankie takes a turn, Johnson is getting kinda
nervous, I say to him, *Fuck you.* Fuckin' pansy. Now Frankie
says, The hell with bowling, let's party. And we're in this
now, so we drive out to the forest preserve, which is always
good for a little privacy, and we put it to her again. Johnson
too this time. Well by now this person, the woman, was
quite distressed, she's, Oh let me go, please let me go, I won't
tell anybody. Only the problem is, she's seen our faces, she
knows who we are. And this is a dilemma. Well I always
carry this hunting knife strapped to my leg, so we took her
into the woods and we—you know—we did what we had to
do. All three taking turns so we were equal.

The Red Address

Blood was everywhere, man. You never seen so much friggin' blood. On the leaves, on the pathway, on our clothes, on our boots. Everything is *red*. Maybe if we had never had all that beer right on top of breakfast it never woulda happened like that. Or if there was something real to do around this goddamn town. Or if she hadn'ta been wearing this outfit, got me all turned on. I mean—the hell was she doing going into a mall at ten o'clock in the morning anyway? Or maybe if I'da waited and gotten my rocks off with the ninth grader, or maybe if fucking Inky had shown up when he was supposed to . . . All these things! You see what I'm saying? There were all these *circumstances*.

I will tell you this: I knew this was gonna happen. I'm not talking about the details, but I been waiting for this. And you know why? 'Cause I'm psychic. Yes, sir, I got second sight. They did some tests on me one time in juvenile detention, I read thirty out of fifty-two cards, blindfold. Ace, king, jack, deuce. I got X-ray eyes. I can *see* things. Like one time I was sitting on a park bench and there was this pigeon there on the sidewalk. Just this ugly gray pigeon, picking up the crumbs, and the seeds . . . And I'm sitting there looking at this bird, all of a sudden—all of a sudden I could see right into it. Like right *into* this bird. I could see so far, I could see the heart inside of it, beating away. This tiny red heart, pumping and pumping . . . So red it was almost black. Have you ever seen anything like that? No, sir, I would bet not. And you know what it's like inside there? It's dark, sir. It's dark inside our bodies. I mean, it's kinda weird for us to be out walking around in daylight, because inside of us, it's always night. Yes, sir. It's always nighttime inside the body. Till somebody cuts you open and lets the daylight in.

Do you see what I'm saying here?

The scene changes.

SCENE FIVE

Office. Another red apple on the desk. Dick and Ann. Dick is signing letters.

DICK Okay. This can go out. (*He hands it to her and signs another.*) This one can go.

ANN Mr. Braverman, are you sure that—

DICK Look. Don't worry about it. (*Signs another one*) This one can go. And send that one registered mail.

ANN I'm sure Mr. Triplett would want to see these letters—

DICK Mr. Triplett is not gonna be *around*. The man just went into mourning. And we got a business to shore up here.

ANN All right. Next letter?

E. G. enters, carrying his briefcase.

E. G. What's going on around here?

ANN Mr. Triplett . . .

DICK E. G . . . ! What the hell are you doing here?

E. G. How is everybody?

DICK E. G, what the fuck are you doing here?

E. G. What does it look like? I'm coming back to work. Annie, have you got the chronological?

ANN Yes, it's right here, Mr. Triplett.

E. G. And today's printout? Have you got that on hand?

ANN Yes, sir. It's right here.

E. G. What is this? (*Picks up the apple from the desk*) Where did this come from?

DICK The what, the apple . . . ?

E. G. Annie, would you take this away, please?

ANN Yes, sir.

E. G. No—never mind. Never mind. It's fine. We'll leave it there.—Just, let me have that printout, so I can see what's going on.

Ann gives him the printout but remains in the room.

DICK E. G., you're really coming back to work?

E. G. Yeah. What's the matter?

DICK Nothing. I'm just a little surprised is all . . .

E. G. This is my business. I shouldn't be here running my business?

DICK No, I think it's great. I just mean—so soon?

E. G. So soon—? What do you mean, so soon.

DICK Well you coulda taken a coupla days. You know, a decent interval.

E. G. Annie—you still there?—listen, I've got a bunch of things boxed up over at the house. Nine or ten boxes. Look up a good trucking company, have them take it all away, will you?

ANN And they should take them—where?

E. G. I don't know. Maybe the Salvation Army, Red Cross. I don't care what they do with 'em.

ANN And what's in these boxes, is this . . .?

E. G. It's women's effects. Clothing, shoes, jewelry, and so on. And ASAP on that, please. I'd like 'em gone today.

ANN   Yes sir.

E. G.   And will you get me Mr. Boyle, please, when you have a chance.

ANN   I'm very sorry about your wife, Mr. Triplett.

Pause.

E. G.   Oh. Yeah. Thank you.

ANN   I didn't know her well but she always seemed like a very nice person.

E. G.   Yeah, well. Thank you.

ANN   If there's anything I can do, here, or at your home, or anyth—

E. G.   —No, I think everything's taken care of, Annie. I think everything is under control. Thanks.

ANN   Anyway. Welcome back to work.

E. G.   Thank you, Ann.

Ann exits.

DICK   Well I say this is great. This is fucking *great,* you coming in like this, and bouncing back? Take-Charge Triplett, huh.

E. G.   Yeah, yeah. What's going on around here? (*He starts looking through a file.*)

DICK   Not too much. The usual. You know. Invoices. Lots of invoices. But hey, Eej, are you sure you're ready to dig back in so soon?

E. G.   Yeah, sure.

The Red Address

DICK How come you didn't take a vacation? How come you didn't go sit under a palm tree and watch some dancing girls?

E. G. Was I here? Was I here already . . . ?

DICK What's that, Eej?

E. G. (*Takes a letter from the file*) A letter to Boyle. What is this . . . ?

DICK Oh yeah, that.

E. G. "If we do not receive immediate payment, we will take legal action. Sincerely, E. G. Triplett . . ."

DICK Yeah, I think there should be an invoice attached . . .

E. G. But this is over my name. It says "E. G. Triplett" here.

DICK Yeah, I thought I should follow right up on that.

E. G. So, you wrote this.

DICK Yeah.

E. G. You wrote a letter to Boyle and you signed my name to it?

DICK Well the receipts were down, I figured you weren't going to be around for a while, so I should take some action. Put a little muscle on these deadbeats.

E. G. Who do you think you are, anyway?

DICK Now hang on a second.

E. G. Who the fuck do you think you are? Did I give you power of attorney? Did you think I was never coming back?

DICK Will you listen to me?

E. G. Don't ever sign my name, Dick.

DICK Well I had to do *something*—

E. G. *Ever.* Don't you *ever* sign my name.

DICK Okay. I'm sorry. I didn't know it was gonna be a big deal.

E. G. *Ever.*

DICK Hey, Eej, what the fuck . . . !

E. G. You are not me. I am not you. You are you. I am I.

DICK Okay, okay . . .

E. G. Do you understand that distinction?

DICK You weren't *around*, E. G. And you know maybe you're not aware of it—

E. G. (*From "maybe you're not aware of it"*) What did you think?

DICK Maybe you're not aware of it, E. G., but we got a major hemorrhage on our hands. We lost five buttons just today, gone over to Driver.

E. G. Yeah, what's going on with Driver?

DICK We're losing buttons right and left, that's what's going on. So I thought I could shore things up a little, bring in some cash. Now if you think I did something *wrong*, then you can—

E. G. (*From "then you can"*) Have you sold the company to Driver yet?

DICK —then you can come out and say it, but don't just shit all over me like this.

E. G. This is a business, Dick.

DICK Exactly. This is a business.

E. G.   This is *my* business.

DICK   Oh, this is *your* business?

E. G.   Yes, this is my business and you are not my partner here, you do not make the decisions.

DICK   Just fuck me, E. G. Okay? Just fuck me. This is your business, this is a *dying* business. And you're my best friend, E. G., but I tell you, if you want to drive me out the door, you're doing a fucking good job of it. Yes I know that I am not a partner here. And that I do not make decisions. But if you think I *like* that, if you think I get down on my knees every night and thank God that I am what I am, then you are out of your fucking mind. And just hang onto your hat, buddy. Hang onto your hat, because I might not be that for long. I might not.

E. G.   What are you talking about?

DICK   Nothing. I'm not talking about anything.

E. G.   No, come on. What's going on here?

DICK   Well. This isn't exactly the moment, but, uh . . . Driver made me an offer. To go over to him.

E. G.   And . . . ?

DICK   Don't worry. I turned him down. Of *course* I turned him down. I never even considered it. I'm sorry I brought it up. It's nothing, it was never a question. Anyway, I'm sorry if I did something wrong, I'm sorry I fucked up the letters, I'm sorry if I spoke out of turn. (*E. G. sinks into his chair and looks around himself.*)   You okay? E. G., you okay? Hey, Eej! Yo, E. G.!

E. G.   Yeah, I'm just a little . . .

DICK Can I get you something? You want a cup of coffee? There's fresh made, I'll get you some.

E. G. No. I'm okay. The place looked funny for a second . . . What were we talking about?

DICK The business.

E. G. Business . . .

DICK Yeah. And you want to know something, Eej? About the business? I found out who Driver is. Yeah. I swear to God. And how's this for a nice little surprise: He's not the guy from Chicago. Is that good news? Driver's not Mr. Mob Guy, he's on the up and up. I got a very reliable source prepared to swear to this.

E. G. So who is he . . . ?

DICK Driver? Well, sure, who is anybody? The point is, we know who he *isn't*. You see what I'm saying? So there'd be nothing illegal, there'd be nothing *dishonorable* if you wanted to go in with him. The needle is pointing towards empty, so I don't know what he'd give you, but if he wants the use of your name, he'll give you *some*thing. Maybe even something substantial. You listening to me? E. G.?

E. G. You know, my wife is dead. (*Silence*) Lady is dead.

DICK Yeah, sure, Eej. I know that . . .

E. G. Did you ever think, there's no inside to an apple . . . ?

DICK The what . . . ?

E. G. You never see the inside of an apple. There *is* no inside.

DICK Uh-huh.

E. G. I mean you bite in, you bite past the surface, what do you get? You get another surface. And you're still on the outside of the apple. And the more you eat all you're ever gonna get is more surface. And when you eat the apple and the apple is gone, all you ever ate was the surface. You see?

DICK Yeah well sure, I get your drift . . .

E. G. I had to identify her. At this place, downtown. This building. I guess it was there all the time, I never noticed it. Only you know what, Dick?—It wasn't her.

DICK "Wasn't her." What, you mean . . . ?

E. G. That wasn't Lady. That, what they showed me, that was not Lady. They take me this room, they showed me this, this person, on a, one of those hospital carts, and I said, This is not my wife. He says to me, Is this your wife, sir? I said, No. I said, This is not my wife, I don't know who this is, but this is not . . . I said, You bring me my wife. You bring me back my fucking wife. You bring me my fucking wife right *now*. You bring me Lady. Oh Jesus. Jesus. Jesus. Jesus . . .

DICK Eej. Eej.

E. G. So how do I live now? How am I supposed to live?

DICK E. G., listen . . .

E. G. I went to the cemetery today, I was standing by the, by the grave there, I was standing on the surface, you see? And you know how hot it's been, I started thinking, Is it hot down there too, under the ground? Or does the earth make it nice and cool . . .

DICK Jesus Christ, Eej, you *cannot think* about these things!

E. G. And she's not that far away! She's right there, she's just under the surface.

DICK Look, can I offer you some free advice, E. G.?

E. G. She's not that far away . . . !

DICK Can I tell you something? Don't dwell on these things. Don't dwell on these things and don't philosophize, because it's not gonna do you any good.

E. G. What do I do, Dick? What do I do? How do I live?

DICK You know I seen some death in my time, too. You remember when my brother died? I didn't go out of the house for two fucking *months,* I was so upset. But I was sixteen years old then. We're men now, we have to deal with these things. Or my old man? You remember that? I was out on that deal in Springfield, I didn't come back for the fucking funeral, man. I stayed out on the deal. I got those fuckers to sign. And my old man would've been proud of me for it, too. He knew what was what. He woulda said, What, stop everything because of a death? No. So you really want my advice? You want to live? I'll tell you how you live. The first thing is, you settle your worldly affairs. I'm sorry to be so banal, but you gotta get your business in order, E. G.

E. G. My business . . .

DICK Yeah, so let's talk some business for a second.

E. G. Fuck . . .

DICK We gotta get that out of the way.

E. G. Fuck. *Fuck* the business!

DICK Buddy, do you want to be saved? Or do you want to be fucked? Because this business as we know it is gone, E. G. But you can go to Joe Driver—who is not the man from Chicago—and you can get some money to keep it open, and *that* is how you live. You'll be here, I'll be here, Annie. What will have changed?

E. G. Yeah . . .

DICK You don't want to deal with the business now, I understand that. So what do you say I set up a meeting, the two of you sit down, and you settle the deal. Okay? You do not have a choice anymore. I'm sorry. So will you meet with Joe Driver? Will you deal with this?

E. G. Yeah. I'll deal. I'll deal.

DICK Okay. Great. Now all you gotta do in the meantime is, you gotta get some relaxation, pal. You gotta find something to distract yourself or you are gonna implode.

E. G. Yeah, if I could just relax, I could think straight . . .

DICK So what can I do for you, E. G.? No questions asked. You want to shoot pool, you want to get drunk, you need a wide-screen color TV? What is your drug? What do you need?

E. G. I need a bright red dress.

DICK What, you want a girl? I'm not asking any questions, E. G. Just tell me. What can I do for you?

E. G. Nothing. Nothing. I'll deal.

DICK Okay, then, I'll go set this up. You make out a very large deposit slip. Everything is good, buddy. Everything is gonna be great! (*He starts out. Stops*)   And don't forget: You are still the king.

Dick exits. The scene changes.

The Red Address

SCENE SIX

A motel room, configured like the bedroom in Scene 2. A
PROSTITUTE *enters, carrying a purse.*

PROSTITUTE   Okay, what's your pleasure, sweetheart. The
possibilities are endless. (*She sees that she's alone.*)   Hey!
You still there?

E. G. enters with a suitcase.

E. G.   Here I am.

PROSTITUTE   I thought I lost you.

E. G.   I just wanted to get this.

PROSTITUTE   Hold it. Hold it. What's that suitcase? What is
that? You didn't have that bag before. Put it down. (*E. G.
sets down the suitcase.*)   You got some kinda hardware in
there? You know a guy once tried to use a knife on me in
some way and I started screaming—you know that guy is
still in jail? And what is this look?

E. G.   Nothing. You just look like somebody.

PROSTITUTE   I look like everybody, now what's this bag?

E. G.   It's nothing, it's—

PROSTITUTE   Open it. And open it nice and slow or I am
outa here.

E. G.   (*Opens the suitcase and takes out the red dress*)   It's just this.

PROSTITUTE   Okay. It's a dress. Translate for me. You want
me to put that on? Some old girlfriend had that, we're
taking a trip down memory lane?

E. G.   No.

PROSTITUTE So what's the . . . ? Oh *shit*.

E. G. That's all I want to do.

PROSTITUTE God*damn* it. Why is it always me?

E. G. I swear. That's all I want, I just want to—

PROSTITUTE You just want to what.

E. G. I just want to talk for a while.

PROSTITUTE Yeah, you want to talk and put on your party outfit, is that all you want here?

E. G. That's all.

PROSTITUTE Well I'm sorry but I don't do men in skirts. Talk to Marie, she specializes. I'll tell you where to find her.

E. G. Please. Please.

PROSTITUTE I'm not gonna fuck you. Uh-uh. No fuckin' way.

E. G. I'm not asking for that.

PROSTITUTE I'm not gonna fuck you or anything *else* with you. I don't even want to even be in the same *room* with you.

E. G. That's okay. That's all right. I'm not asking for that. You don't have to do anything. Just . . . All I want to do is put this on. I swear.

PROSTITUTE You know this could cost you.

E. G. I know.

PROSTITUTE This could cost you a *lot*.

E. G. I'll pay you. Name your price. Anything.

PROSTITUTE   Okay. So put on your dress. Slip into a ball gown, Harry. What the fuck do *I* care? (*E. G. takes stockings and the red high heels out of the suitcase.*)   I see we came prepared.

E. G.   Will you do something for me?

PROSTITUTE   What. Don't ask me to fuck you.

E. G.   Will you ask if I want to go to the red address?

PROSTITUTE   Will I ask *what*?

E. G.   Just say, "Do you want to go to the red address."

PROSTITUTE   Okay. Do you want to go to the red address?

E. G.   I do want to go the red address. I do want to go to the red address.

PROSTITUTE   Okay. So?

E. G.   Nothing.

PROSTITUTE   Is this a riddle? Ha ha?

E. G.   No. That's all. (*E. G. starts dressing.*)   Everything's going to be okay now. Everything's going to be fine. I'm on my way to the red address. I'm on my way to the red address . . .

PROSTITUTE   Fuckin' freak show. Boy I tell you, if men fucked as much as they fantasized *around* these days, I'd be dead from overexertion. Because there seems to be a general decline in simple fucking and general rise in extracurricular bullshit like this—at least from my limited perspective. Sex toys and lots of talk, that's what little boys are made of. The way diseases are going around, maybe that's a blessing. The way diseases are going around, even the guys who just want to "*talk*" oughta put on a rubber. Okay. The meter is running. What do we want to "talk" about?

E. G. Did you see anything today?

PROSTITUTE I beg your pardon?

E. G. Did you see anything interesting today?

PROSTITUTE Are you kidding? I woke up at 7 P.M. and fucked twenty-five men, how's that? You want details? Just. Hey. One question. About the larger picture. Are you the exception, getting dressed up like this, or are you part of some greater historical trend?

E. G. I don't know.

PROSTITUTE I mean, did stupid cunts like me have to put up with this in Roman times, or is it new?

E. G. I don't know.

PROSTITUTE I don't know either.

E. G. Men are going to be extinct in a few thousand years anyway.

PROSTITUTE Can't happen soon enough, if you ask me.

E. G. Maybe in the future all men will wear stockings and high heels.

PROSTITUTE It can't happen soon enough . . . Far as I'm concerned nylon stockings are a major pain in the ass and the guy who invented 'em oughta rot in the seventh circle of hell, so if men want to wear 'em, go ahead, let 'em suffer. They say hookers are gonna go extinct someday. I can't wait . . . But hey. Second question. You don't have to answer. Are you married? (*E. G. says nothing.*) Hello?

E. G. I was married . . .

PROSTITUTE You always are. You guys always are. And it's always the same story. "My wife don't understand me." Or, "My girlfriend don't understand me." Or this: "My wife can't sympathize with my desire to put on a brassiere." Jesus! Was that in the marriage contract? I promise to love, honor, and obey and let you wear my *bras*—?

E. G. *I* saw something today.

PROSTITUTE You realize I could have a very easy time of it, blackmailing you right now. This town isn't that big. You're probably a businessman, some kind of entrepreneur? For all you know, I got a movie camera hidden in here.

E. G. I don't think I care anymore.

PROSTITUTE I could be taking pictures.

E. G. I don't care anymore.

PROSTITUTE Terrific. Go and God bless, get yourself a life and get offa my fucking back, Tom.

E. G. I saw a nice outfit today.

PROSTITUTE The what?

E. G. I saw this outfit in a shop window. A long green skirt and a—

PROSTITUTE Just cut it with the girl talk, okay? Just cut it. (*Short pause*) You got a runner.

E. G. Will you help me into this? (*She says nothing, just looks at him.*) Please? (*She does up the back of his dress.*) If you were a man you'd probably blackmail me.

PROSTITUTE Oh you think so.

E. G. Women are more understanding than men.

PROSTITUTE Oh, sure. Sure. "Understanding." Tell that to Lizzie Borden. Tell that to Lucretia Borgia.

E. G. You didn't have to do this.

PROSTITUTE I am getting *paid* to do this, brother. I'm sure as fuck not doing it for fun. Understanding equals economics, in case you haven't heard.

E. G. I don't believe that.

PROSTITUTE So believe whatever you want. You're paying.

E. G. Do you mind if I walk a little?

PROSTITUTE Brother, you can do whatever you want. You're paying.

E. G. (*Pacing the room*) Everything's good now. Everything's okay. Everything's okay . . .

PROSTITUTE At least this is a relief from some of the other shit I have to put up with from you creatures. Like the CPA who calls me up three times a week so he can tie me down and shoot his come all over my face? You think that's fun? This is a Methodist picnic, compared. Or the high school gym coach who likes to use me for his punching bag? I lost a fucking tooth back here last week. I oughta make him pay for it.

E. G. Yeah, but there has to be . . .

PROSTITUTE I beg your pardon? Excuse me?

E. G. I was gonna say, there has to be something you can do.

PROSTITUTE Oh, yeah, like what? Maybe you think I can turn this guy down when he drives up in his Buick Skylark and tells me he wants to fuck me? This guy weighs two hundred and sixty pounds, he's a fucking *gym* coach. You think I want to *die*? And you know why he likes to pick me up so often?

He says it's because he *likes* me. Yeah, maybe if he didn't "like" me so much I could live a little longer. You fucking men. You are not a sex. You are not a gender. You are a fucking weapon pointed at women's heads. Do you know that?

E. G.   I do know that—

PROSTITUTE   No you do not know that, because you are not a *woman*. I don't give a fuck what kinda clothes you're wearing. You cannot *know*. I am *telling* you.

E. G.   I'm sorry.

PROSTITUTE   You're sorry. *I'm* sorry. Excuse me, I gotta do something. I need some help here . . . (*She takes a pill bottle from her bag and downs a few.*)   Fuck. Fuck . . . (*She stands still a moment, waiting for the rush.*)   Sweet Jesus.

E. G.   Do you want some water?

PROSTITUTE   Huh?

E. G.   Some water.

PROSTITUTE   Nah, it's okay, it's okay. It's that time of night, is all. Coupla minutes on these things, I'll feel like a million bucks.

E. G.   (*Looking at himself in the mirror*)   Am I fucked? Or am I saved . . .

PROSTITUTE   Say what?

E. G.   Putting on these clothes. Am I fucked or am I saved?

PROSTITUTE   You're sure not gonna get fucked by me, pal. I like those shoes.

E. G.   Aren't they pretty?

PROSTITUTE   Yeah. Very sharp. Straight outa *Redbook*.

E. G. My wife bought these.

PROSTITUTE Excuse me?

E. G. My wife bought these for me.

PROSTITUTE So she knows about you doing this? What the fuck are you doing *here*? Go bug *her*! (*Realizes*) Oh yeah. You said. (*E. G. says nothing.*) You divorced, or . . . ?

E. G. No, she uh . . . She died.

PROSTITUTE That's tough. Any kids?

E. G. No. No kids.

PROSTITUTE That's very tough.—You want a drink? I got a bottle.

E. G. No thanks.

PROSTITUTE Some pills? There's plenty.

E. G. Will you do something else?

PROSTITUTE What.

E. G. Will you say it's beautiful?

PROSTITUTE What's beautiful.

E. G. Just say, "It's beautiful."

PROSTITUTE Okay. It's beautiful.

E. G. Say it again.

PROSTITUTE It's beautiful. It's beautiful. Like that? It's beautiful. It's beautiful.

E. G. What do I do, Lady?

PROSTITUTE Say what?

E. G. How do I live?

PROSTITUTE Fast as possible, pal.

E. G. How do I live?

PROSTITUTE Well aside from the dress—unless you don't see the dress as a problem.

E. G. I always liked the way this dress sounds. The whisper it makes when I move. Do you hear that whisper?

PROSTITUTE You know, my brother, he used to do this. My brother Tommy. He liked to dress up.

E. G. How do you know?

PROSTITUTE I caught him wearing my stuff, that's how I know. And I know where this got started, too. Nine years old, can you believe it?

E. G. I can believe that.

PROSTITUTE His class at school wants to put on this play. *Little Red Riding Hood.* Sounds pretty harmless, right? Only his teacher—one of these, you know, "creative" teachers— she puts the names of all the characters in a hat, and you had to reach into this hat and take out a piece of paper to see what part you were gonna play. Well Tommy, he reaches in and he gets this piece of paper that says "Emily" on it. Meaning he had to play a girl.

E. G. And that was the start.

PROSTITUTE Well, oh man did he fight about this. Did he scream, I remember. But my mother gives him one of my old dresses, the teacher finds him this blond wig. I still remember him sitting in his room in this costume, screaming how nobody was gonna make him go out in public like that.

Then I come home one day I find him walking around the house in my party dress. I practically *shit*. He's got on the stilettos, and the eye shadow, the good stockings . . .

E. G. He was hooked.

PROSTITUTE He was hooked. Weird thing is, the stuff looked kinda good on him. Tommy swears me to silence, next thing I know I'm lending him my stuff so's he could walk around the house. Could hardly keep the little bastard *outa* my stuff. And all this because he reaches into a hat one day and pulls out a piece of paper that says "Emily." Or who knows. Maybe it was in his chromosomes or something. Whatever happens, *has* to happen. That's what this friend of mine says. Everything that happens has to happen . . .

E. G. I kept trying to throw this stuff out.

PROSTITUTE That was just like him. Always hiding it, so nobody'd know.

E. G. I'd box it up and carry it out to the curb—five minutes later I'd go out and bring it back in. Then I'd put it back out in the garbage—ten minutes later I'd go out and take it back in again.

PROSTITUTE Always hiding it . . .

E. G. So where is he now?

PROSTITUTE The what . . . ?

E. G. Your brother. What happened to him?

PROSTITUTE Tommy? I don't know where Tommy is. He prob'ly joined the army. He's prob'ly in jail someplace. Multiple murder or something . . . Only what the hell is wrong with these pills? I'm not getting no buzz, here. Anyway what's it to you? Fuck you. Who asked you?

E. G. Look, I didn't mean to—

PROSTITUTE Just fuck off, okay? Forget I ever opened my mouth. Fucking pervert. Yeah, what kinda black hat did *you* reach into? And what the fuck is wrong with goddamn pills? I musta gotten some dummies . . . (*Rummages in her bag for more*) Boy, you are really fucked, do you know that? Carrying around a bagful of women's clothes from place to place. You think *that's* a way to live? Huh? Huh?

E. G. No.

PROSTITUTE You wanna go back and forth to the garbage forever and ever? Trying to throw your dress out and taking it back in? Hiding out?

E. G. No.

PROSTITUTE You know you don't get no second chance at that hat, little boy. You don't get no second piece of paper with some different name on it. This outfit here? This is your *fate,* baby. This is you.

E. G. This is me.

PROSTITUTE Yeah, so get used to it. Now can we settle up and get outa here? This place is spooking the shit outa me.

E. G. (*Hands her money*) Here.

PROSTITUTE Whoa, whoa! Too much.

E. G. No, keep it. Thank you.

PROSTITUTE Okay, well. Don't let anybody tell you different. But you are a real gentleman.

Prostitute exits. E. G. looks at himself in the mirror. The scene changes.

SCENE SEVEN

Restaurant. Driver and Dick.

DRIVER   I can't wait here all damn day, Dick.

DICK   I know that, Joe, and we're trying to remedy the situation as best as we can.

DRIVER   When I say noon, I mean noon.

DICK   This is very unlike E. G. The man is pathologically prompt. But you know he's been under a lot of stress lately.

DRIVER   I know he's been under stress but that's no excuse for letting your whole goddamn business go to hell.

DICK   Goddamn right it's no excuse, but you can depend on E. G. that there is some kinda good solid reason for this. When he and I discussed this meeting, he was very tractable, he was all ready to do business.

DRIVER   I will give him two minutes.

Ann enters.

ANN   Mr. Braverman.

DICK   Excuse me, Joe. (*Steps aside with Ann*)   So where is he?

ANN   I don't know. He didn't call the office and he's not at home.

DICK   Check the machine.

ANN   I just checked it. He didn't leave a message.

DICK   You told him noon.

ANN   I told him noon, I told him the place.

DICK   Did you go to his house?

ANN   I went there, I rang the bell, I must've knocked for ten minutes at least.

DICK   You didn't go into the house?

ANN   No, I just knocked and—

DICK   Annie, you go to the office, you get the extra key to his house, and you go in and you check on him.

ANN   But I can't just walk into Mr. Triplett's house—

DICK   This is a guy on the edge. Who *knows* what the hell is wrong here.

DRIVER   I will wait one more minute, Dick!

DICK   It's all taken care of, Joe. (*To Ann*)   If we have to, we call the police, have 'em put out an APB. Now go.

MAÎTRE D' (*Offstage*)   You cannot go out there. Excuse me, sir, but you cannot go out there—! Sir? Sir? Sir?

E. G. enters in a dress and high heels, carrying a briefcase and a shopping bag that says "SOUVENIR." He is accompanied by the MAITRE D'.

E. G.   Afternoon, everybody.

DICK   *Jesus!*

MAÎTRE D'   Sir, you are going to have to leave.

E. G.   How is everyone today?

DICK   Jesus . . .

ANN   Oh my God . . . !

E. G.   Sorry I cut it this close. I had to pick up a few things on the way. How are you, Dick?

DICK   Jesus!

The Red Address

MAÎTRE D' Sir, you are going to have to leave right now or I will call the police.

E. G. I come in here all the time.

MAÎTRE D' Will you come with me, please?

E. G. The owner knows me—why don't you ask him? Ann, how are you?

ANN Oh my God . . .

MAÎTRE D' All right, then, I'm calling the police.

Maître d' exits.

E. G. Afternoon, Joe.

DRIVER Well, hello there, E. G.

E. G. How are you?

DRIVER I'm good, I'm good. Question seems to be, how are *you* today?

E. G. I'm superior, thank you.

DRIVER Uh-huh.

DICK E. G.—what the fuck is going on here?! Is this a joke, or—what is this?

E. G. Is what a joke?

DICK Well, do you realize you are wearing a *dress*?

E. G. Yeah. I'm wearing a dress.

DICK So could you . . . Uh-huh. Uh-huh.

E. G. Ann, would you find the waiter, please? We're going to have some lunch.

ANN   Yes, Mr. Triplett.

Ann exits.

DICK   Joe, I don't know what the hell is going on here. I swear to God.

DRIVER   Well, that is a mighty pretty outfit you got on there, Mr. Triplett. Is this in my honor?

E. G.   No, it's just something for the office.

DRIVER   I see.

DICK   I swear to God, Joe.

E. G.   Are you ready to do business, Joe?

DRIVER   I'm always ready to do business.

E. G.   Great. (*E. G. opens his purse and takes out a deck of cards. He throws it onto the table.*)   My cards are on the table. Want to draw?

DRIVER   Why am I getting this funny déjà vu feeling, all of a sudden? And how do I know you're playing with a full deck? So to speak.

E. G.   Check the cards yourself. Crack open a fresh one, if you think it'll make a difference.

DRIVER   You don't think we're still playing for ten million dollars, do you, honey?

E. G.   All right. Why don't we make it a dollar. I get the high card, we're partners for a dollar, I get the low card— nothing's changed.

DRIVER   You are very cocky today, are you not?

E. G.   The cards are still on the table.

DRIVER   Okay. Let's draw. (*They each draw a card and show it.*)   Well, well, well.

E. G.   Looks like we're back where we started. So if you want my business you're going to have to run me *out* of business.

DRIVER   Is that so.

E. G.   And you're going to have to work pretty hard, because I plan to triple my business this year.

DRIVER   Mr. Triplett, what would I do with your business now even if I wanted it? Now that your name is worth jack *shit* around this town. I couldn't run you outa business half so well as you're running yourself.

E. G.   Is that so.

DRIVER   You're making things too easy on me.

E. G.   Is that so.

DRIVER   Maybe with this kinda luck, I ought think about pulling up stakes here. I have accomplished just about everything I could here.

E. G.   So if there's nothing more to say, then—what's to say?

DRIVER   You still don't know who I am, do you, son.

E. G.   I think I know what you are.

DRIVER   DID YOU THINK THAT YOU COULD FUCK WITH ME, MR. TRIPLETT? AND DO YOU *STILL* THINK THAT YOU CAN FUCK WITH ME?

E. G.   I do what I can.

DRIVER   You are a brave man, E. G.

Driver exits.

E. G. (*Taking a paper out of his briefcase*) I figured it out, Dick. We're not going out of business. We're expanding the business. First thing is, we go out to all the customers and we offer them a discount. Maybe 5 percent, 10 percent, we can talk about it.

DICK A discount.

E. G. We have to be nicer to our customers, Dick. Do you want some lunch?

DICK E. G., have you gone queer or something?

E. G. No, I haven't gone queer.

DICK Okay, so can you *explain*?

E. G. There's nothing to explain.

DICK I mean the outfit?

E. G. I dress like this all the time.

DICK Oh. Oh—you dress like this all the time.

E. G. That's right.

DICK Well not in *public* you don't dress like—Okay. Okay. Maybe you dress like this at home, behind closed curtains or something. Maybe that's your personal kink. But . . . the maintenance of civilization depends on . . . the observance of certain proprieties!

E. G. What's the difference if I wear this instead of a jacket and tie?

DICK There *is* a difference, E. G.

E. G. It's just clothing.

DICK No, this is not just clothing. This is—not clothing. This is . . .

E. G. Have you ever tried on a dress, Dick?

DICK No, I have never tried on a dress.

E. G. Maybe you tried on some of Theodora's things when she wasn't—

DICK *I have never put on a dress.* Okay? Now will you please go change so we can talk? So I can at least *look* at you?

E. G. What am I hurting by wearing this?

DICK You're hurting *me,* all right? I don't even know who the fuck I'm *talking* to right now! Who are you?

E. G. This is me. And I'm free now, Dick.

DICK Oh. You're free.

E. G. That's right.

DICK No. You are not free now. You're disturbed, E. G. You're inside out. You need help.

E. G. You told me to do what I had to do. No questions asked.

DICK I am so ashamed of you, E. G. I am so fucking ashamed. And how are you gonna deal with this now?

E. G. I've dealt.

DICK What, in this town? No, no, you have not dealt. You know this town, E. G. You have not *begun* to deal. And you think you're gonna run a business like this?

E. G. I'm going to try.

DICK   Do you think people are even gonna want to *see* you like this? And work with you? Do you think that *I* want anything to do with you, like this?

E. G.   I'm sorry you feel that way.

DICK   Oh, you're sorry I feel this way.

E. G.   No, I mean—I'm sorry, Dick.

DICK   You're sorry. That's beautiful. Well, you are out of your fucking mind. And you just take a good look at this face, buddy. Because this is the last time you are ever gonna see it. You want to talk to me, you call Joe Driver's number. You fucking pussy.

E. G.   Dick . . .

DICK   You fucking *faggot*. Jesus! Jesus!

Dick exits. Ann enters.

ANN   Mr. Triplett . . .

E. G.   Annie. Yeah. Do you want some lunch? It's on the company. We can do some work.

ANN   Actually, I think I'd better get back to the office.

E. G.   Maybe later on you could help me buy a few things, help me pick out something to wear.

ANN   I don't think so.

E. G.   I'll need some skirts and blouses, a few dresses . . .

ANN   I don't think so.

E. G.   I'd love to get your advice.

ANN   I'm sorry, I—I just don't think so.

E. G.   Oh. All right. Okay. Well, thank you, Ann.

ANN   Will that be all?

E. G.   Yes, I think that's all. Thank you. That's all.

Ann exits. The Maître d' enters.

MAÎTRE D'   The police are on their way.

E. G.   Good. Maybe they'll want some lunch. Can I see a menu, please? (*He takes out papers to work. The Maître d' stays.*) I'm going to wait here till I get it. Thank you.

The scene changes.

Scene Eight

Bar. A single red light on a barstool. Dick sits there in a winter coat.

DICK   You know the guy I'm talking about. King of the Businessman's Basketball Team. Former touch football star. He used to come in here all the time. Back when he was still wearing a fucking suit and tie. You prob'ly heard how everybody jumped ship over at his company. *I* sure bailed outa there fast. And his secretary, Annie, she was right behind me. I mean, who is gonna do business with a guy in a skirt? I got a living to make, myself, I got a wife to support. But that fucker, he would not give up. He kept that office open, he practically lived at that office. Still making calls, in the high heels. Annie kept up with him, she'd call him up from time to time, see how he was doing, talk for a while. She said he always seemed *happy,* anyhow. Great, I said to her. Let him be happy. Fucking lunatic . . .

   Anyway one day Annie calls me up, she says she can't reach him. She went to his office a few times, she called his house, she can't locate him anywhere. I said to her, Big deal, maybe he's outa town, maybe he went to the South Seas. Maybe he got married to a weight lifter. But Annie's all worried, she wants this and she wants that, I say to her, Look, I don't want to hear about it. Fucking faggot, let him rot. I got no time anyway, looking for a job, *my* problem being I believe you should be nice to your customers— something which is unacceptable in the current climate. I mean how is a person supposed to live? How do you live? Only what it turns out, in the end . . .

Turns out he was in the morgue. Yeah. All this time he was in a freezer in the fucking morgue. They found him in the river. Not even here—like way the hell downriver, so he's all the way over in like the next *county*. They find this naked body, unidentifiable. They stick him in a drawer. Case unsolved, sixty days unclaimed in a drawer, they're taking him out to give him a public burial—when Annie finds this out. Only who knows? Maybe it wasn't even him, right? I mean, nobody went down and *identified* him. We just . . . we showed up for this, uh, this funeral today.

Some cemetery you never even *heard* of, way the fuck out in . . . I don't know. And you know how cold it's been, I don't know how they dug up the fucking ground to make the hole. Musta used a . . . Anyway we get there and there's this, this box. Just a . . . in the back of a station wagon. This plywood box.

Do you know how they bury you on the public money? You know what you get? You get a wooden box, buddy, with a number written on it in *pencil*. And this little marker with a number so if they ever have to dig you up they'll know where to find you. That is the whole extent of it.

E. G. crosses the stage behind Dick in a pool of light, then exits.

Anyway. This funeral. Annie and me are standing around freezing our asses off, pretty soon this priest shows up, this—this fucking *weasel,* this . . . I mean *he* didn't know who he was burying there. I could tell by the look on his face. I bet this guy was getting paid by the funeral, like fucking piecework to bury these anonymous bodies. He just wanted to stay warm in his Lincoln Town Car till the last minute so he could read the prayers and get it over with and go back home.

And when he finally comes up to the, you know, the grave there and this box is sitting there on the bands over the hole—Annie and me and the gravedigger, we're the whole fucking congregation. Where are all his friends? Huh? Where is Marbella, who he set up in business, where is Dorff, who he did a thousand favors for, where is Johnson, where is Panko, where is Boyle, whose ass he saved from bankruptcy? Where are the people whose charity he contributed to year after year every holiday, Christian or Moslem or Jew? And then this guy, this priest, comes up to the grave with his prayerbook and he says—he didn't even know the first fucking thing!—the priest stands there, he says, "Was this a man or a woman? I need to know for the purpose of the prayers." And I said to him—I said—"Was this a . . . ?" This fucking pasty-faced weasel, I grabbed that prayerbook outa his hand, I said to him, "This was a man, motherfucker. *This was a man.* And he was my friend. His name was E. G. Triplett." Amen.

The lights fade.

END OF PLAY